PREPARING
EXPOSITORY
SERMONS

THE SCRIPTURE SCULPTURE PROCESS

PREPARING
EXPOSITORY
SERMONS

A Seven-Step Method for Biblical Preaching

RAMESH RICHARD

Baker Books

A Division of Baker Book House Co
Grand Rapids, Michigan 49516

Published by Baker Books
a division of Baker Book House Company
P.O. Box 6287, Grand Rapids, MI 49516-6287

Fourth printing, February 2005

Revised edition of *Scripture Sculpture*

Printed in the United States of America

Library of Congress Cataloging-in-Publication Data

Richard Ramesh, 1953–
    Preparing expository sermons : a seven-step method for biblical preaching / Ramesh Richard.
        p.   cm.
    Rev. ed. of: Scripture sculpture. ©1995
    Includes bibliographical references and index.
    ISBN 0-8010-9119-5 (pbk)
    1. Preaching. 2. Bible—Homiletical use. I. Richard, Ramesh, 1953- Scripture sculpture. II. Title.

BV4211.2.R52   2001
251´.01—dc22   2001037637

For current information about all releases from Baker Book House, visit our web site:
http://www.bakerbooks.com

Dedication

To my father,
the Rev. Dr. D. John Richard,
who works hard at
preaching and teaching
God's Word
with skillful words.

He is worthy of double honor.

1 Timothy 5:17

Acknowledgments

Since iron sharpens iron, special thanks go to my colleagues in the Pastoral Ministries department of Dallas Theological Seminary and to my preaching seminar hosts in several countries. The former constitute the academic laboratory for this homiletical system; the latter gather preachers to test the method in the practical realities of pulpit ministry.

CONTENTS

Preface   9

Introduction
Motivation, Definition, and Overview of the Process   15

The Scripture Sculpture Process
1 Study the Text   33
   The "Flesh" of the Text
2 Structure the Text   53
   The "Skeleton" of the Text
3 The Central Proposition of the Text   65
   The "Heart" of the Text
4 The Purpose Bridge   77
   The "Brain" of the Sermon
5 The Central Proposition of the Sermon   85
   The "Heart" of the Sermon
6 Structure the Sermon   95
   The "Skeleton" of the Sermon
7 Preach the Sermon   129
   The "Flesh" of the Sermon

Afterword   141

Appendices
1 The Holy Spirit and Your Pulpit Effectiveness   145
2 The Benefits of the Original Languages for Preachers   151

  3 Choosing a Text for Your Sermon   153
  4 Introductory Notes on Grammar   155
  5 The Perils of Principilization   160
  6 Hermeneutical Analysis and Homiletical Application of Narrative Texts   165
  7 Central Propositions: An Advanced Procedure   172
  8 Understanding Your Audience: Exegeting Culture   180
  9 The Elements of a Competent Sermon Outline   184
 10 A Sample Sermon Introduction   186
 11 Forms of Sermon Introduction   191
 12 Sermon Evaluation Questionnaire   193
 13 Topical Exposition   198

     Notes   204
     Bibliography   213
     Scripture Index   216

PREFACE

"All my best thoughts have been stolen by the ancients!" complained Emerson. I have found his saying to be truer of presenting a sequence for sermon preparation than of any other topic in which I have dabbled. This ancient robbery happened on the highway of intellectual traffic even before I was born. How else can the rhetorical practice and the homiletical impact of a Chrysostom, an Augustine, an Aquinas, a Zwingli, a Calvin, a Knox, a Baxter, a Wesley, a Brooks, or a Spurgeon be explained except they robbed from me?[1] Further, they did not even acknowledge the eventual source of their thoughts on preaching. Highway robbery victims at least know they have been robbed. I did not know it was happening to me. Life is unjust.

After convicting the ancients of stealing my thoughts, I look at my contemporaries and charge them with telepathic advantages. In an excessively competitive academic and publishing environment, my older professors and wiser colleagues read my thoughts, packaged them, and promoted them before I had an opportunity to publish them. They seized what I wanted to say and presented it in much better form. I am now made to look as though I took it from them. How else can one explain the superb homiletical writings or the pulpit energy of a host of contemporary pastors and preachers? Again, I am the loser. Life is unfair.

Airing my grievances to you my reader already provides relief! But it will not absolve me from responsibility in the following pages.

More than six hundred titles on preaching occupy the BV4211 area of the Turpin Library at Dallas Seminary. When we add the journals and articles that are dedicated to the dynamics and mechanics of preaching, the total exceeds one thousand productions of recent history (384 B.C. [Aristotle]—A.D. 2001). I have examined most of them and know this book is not an unaffected contribution to the homiletical enterprise. It may actually begin the regressive dice roll of homiletical theory and practice. Since life is unfair and unjust to all, however, the masters have to put up with my little sayings on the matter.

The philosophy and praxis of this "patchwork of plagiarisms"[2] is being fashioned out of a twenty-five-year chronology of personal imperfections. The book really began in teenage open-air preaching experiences in the market streets of Madras, South India. At this formative time of life, I was exposed to the effective preaching of my pastor, Samuel Kamaleson, at the Emmanuel Methodist Church. The encouragement of teenage peers as we preached on sand beaches and electric trains counted toward this book. The consistent lifestyle of my father, John Richard—who loves Christ, the ministry, and books—gave me an advantageous heritage.

At Dallas Seminary I was forced to enhance the gift of preaching. Gracious professors legislated and affirmed my preaching experiences. I will never forget Haddon Robinson's comment after a rather difficult space/time event called "Introduction to Expository Preaching 603." He said, "Mr. Richard, I had no burning desire to listen to you!" Was this possibly a stimulus to improve my preparation and preaching?

The responses of my congregation to the pulpit-oriented pastorate of Delhi Bible Fellowship, North India, reinforced the calling to exalt preaching as the central weekly event of church life. One family who had to move to Bombay wrote: "Bombay is milder climate-wise, denser population-wise and more orderly bus-wise. But I will be missing the fellowship and the weekly living sermons. I have attended a couple of church services here, but if you will allow me to say so, the preaching here is like taking a beer after a good scotch whiskey. P.S. Sorry to use a comparison you do not have the benefit of having experienced."[3]

The ministry blossomed, and the burgeoning need for Bible study leaders forced me to teach the preaching process to budding young men every week. Some of these have developed into excellent pulpiteers.

Extensive international preaching opportunities exposed me to large audiences of pastors and church leaders who have to minister weekly and often to multiple congregations. These have had little or no formal training in preaching but must preach. They are called, gifted, and appointed to the task. Was there any way I could take the process to them? Was there a simplified and cross-culturally adaptable sermon-preparation process applicable across literary genres and literacy levels that could be imparted to them?

Dallas Seminary gives me another opportunity. As a homiletically inclined institution, it provides me a laboratory where I can keep the issues defined and applied with upcoming pastors and preachers. Ramesh Richard Evangelism and Church Helps (RREACH) International provides the resources to equip pastors, preachers, and thinkers in economically deprived regions with pulpit skills, study tools, and ministry resources.

On this organizationally symbiotic platform, I have put together a seven-step sermon-shaping process for pastors and leaders in needy countries. Since it has been forged out of the foibles of hundreds of seminary students and thousands of pastors at Scripture Sculpture seminars all over the world, I know what must not be done with the text or in the pulpit! Hopefully, I have converted personal imperfections and student shortcomings into a positive format. I have been gratified by the response of preachers in varied cultures who think they have received a process that may be consistently used for their pulpit ministry week after week.

What is also gratifying is the response of fourth-year seminary students who feel that in this format three years of excellent homiletical preparation are summarized and unified for weekly ministry.[4] This manual was not explicitly written for experienced pulpiteers, but I believe even they would find it useful.

The work is divided into three parts. The introduction presents the motivation for expository preaching as well as a definition and an overview of the expository preaching process. The Scripture

Sculpture process is delineated in seven steps. They can stand alone as a do-it-yourself manual on expository preaching. These chapters also suggest "action steps" for you to take. For best comprehension of the proposed method, it is necessary to actually and quickly pursue the action steps. Keep your pencil handy. Read slowly and intentionally. Make notes in the margins of this manual or in a notebook designated for this study. The third part of this book, the appendices, deals with specific (introductory and technical) issues and may be consulted as you see a need for them while working through steps 1 through 7.

Like any other skill, learning to preach will entail effort, concentration, and practice. I desire the sermon-sculpting process to become second nature to you. I want you to be able to apply it without having to think about it. I suggest the following strategy to teach yourself this system.

Choose a biblical text you would like to preach in two months' time. Dedicate two hours one day a week for the next seven weeks to apply this method of sermon preparation. Do one step each week. Then choose another text. Compress the seven-step process into three and a half weeks. Finally, do the process in one week. After going through the method about three times, you will find it becoming second nature to you.

Since the majority of pastors are men, I use the masculine pronoun for easier reading. The ideas in this book are for both men and women, and the use of masculine pronouns in no way is meant to demean women's ministries.

INTRODUCTION

MOTIVATION, DEFINITION, AND OVERVIEW OF THE PROCESS

In a curio shop outside the Kwara Hotel in Ilorin, Kwara State, Nigeria, you would find Daniel's exquisite wooden sculptures. An excellent sculptor, he chooses the finest mahogany and transforms it, as he says, into a "thing of beauty (and joy for some) forever."

I had an opportunity to observe Daniel as he carved a piece of wood. In his hands the piece had promise. Wood sculpting is an art and a science. The scientific part of the sculpting technique is shared by all good sculptors. But the art part is needed to create a truly beautiful piece. Each of Daniel's sculptures was an excellent autograph of his artistic gifts, training, and commitment to work.

We struck up a conversation. He described the process brilliantly: "The tree is what God made; the sculpture is what Daniel makes with what God has made."

In that perceptive comment, I find so many parallels to preparing and delivering an expository sermon. The Bible is what God has made; sermons are what we make with what God has made. Many can duplicate the method. Good preachers share common features of study and delivery. As art, however, your sermon is peculiarly

15

> The Bible is what God has made. Sermons are what we make with what God has made.

yours. A combination of gifts, training, and hard work will personalize your work.

There is a difference, of course, between a wooden sculpture and your sermon—life itself! A living tree is transformed into an inert piece of beauty. Your sermon, under the supervision of the living God, transforms the living Word of God into a sermon that conveys, communicates, and creates life in your hearers. Your sermon is more than a thing of beauty and joy forever. It is a thing of life forever.

The Need for Expository Preaching

Unfortunately, some preachers do not believe that the Bible is what God has made. Unconverted preachers occupy pulpits all across our lands. They neither believe the Word of the Lord nor the Lord of the Word. I have constant correspondence with a certain bishop, a dear man of God who is surrounded by unconverted priests. They have threatened to get rid of him because of his evangelical stand. They do not believe the Bible is what God has made.

Some other preachers believe that sermons may be made without the Bible. They pursue a contemporary parable or pulpit-worthy news event. Usually these sermons are found in erudite pulpits with illustrations drawn from sports, music, politics, and culture, but their biblical content is minimal. In a large Asian city, an astute layman lamented the absence of the Bible from his pastor's sermons. "My pastor does not believe the Bible is sophisticated enough for his audience," he said to me. "My pastor does not feed sheep. He addresses giraffes!"

Still other preachers do not believe that preachers must prepare a sermon. They do not work hard toward the pulpit ministry. In an offhanded manner they typically expect to be divinely filled at the threshold of the sermonic moment. A pastor friend who held this philosophy of sermon preparation was in for a rude shock as he waited in the pulpit for a last-minute word from heaven. There was silence. He dialogued with God concerning the divine promise to fill his servants with divine messages. And there was silence. At last, in abject desperation he pleaded, "God, tell me something about this morning's message." And God told him, "Son, you didn't prepare!"

Finally, some preachers have just let go of preaching as the central thrust of their ministry. They have dismissed preaching as a ministry priority and have elevated counseling ministries or organizational leadership or some other pressing agenda to top priority. Preaching the Bible has become secondary in the hierarchy of ministry tasks, and the urgent needs of society extract the primary energy of the preacher.

One morning when a friend returned from attending church, I asked him what the preacher spoke about. He replied that the topic of the Sunday service was "Three Words Every Christian Must Use." "And what were these?" I queried. He answered, "Thank you, please, and I'm sorry."

One does not have to go to church to learn the rules of social etiquette, though to learn them there is quite all right. What preacher has not desired that social courtesy rule at board meetings! If these are the main items on a regular Sunday menu, however, then the church, the pastor, and the congregation will be spiritually famished.

This book is designed to help you overcome the pulpit deficiencies that have been listed above and to invite you to pursue expository preaching as a way of life and ministry.

The Impact of Expository Preaching

Expository preaching will impact your life. It can help you

- grow personally in knowledge and obedience by your disciplined exposure to God's Word
- conserve time and energy used in choosing a sermon for each week
- balance your area of "expertise" and preferred topics with the breadth of God's thoughts in the Bible

Expository preaching will impact your congregation, because it helps you

- be faithful to the text and be relevant to your context in regular ministry
- implement a strategy for equipping and energizing your people for long-term faithfulness to God and the ministry
- overcome your tendency to target a sermon to a particular person or group and be protected from that charge
- avoid skipping over what does not suit your taste or temperament on any given day
- carry on a cohesive ministry in the middle of multiple dimensions and demands on you as a pastor
- enhance the dignity of the pastoral work since you stand under the authority of God's Word as you preach
- integrate the conversation of the church around the message of the week
- communicate the intentions of God for your congregation as seen by its human leaders
- orient people around a common vision, thus helping you surface the voluntary labor force needed to achieve the vision
- motivate people to action in implementing the program of the church with God's sanction
- garner the credibility needed to lead the church to change
- model effective ministry to present and future teachers and preachers
- outline the agenda for corporate spirituality
- make your congregation biblically literate

Basically, expository preaching helps the preacher promote God's agenda for his people.

Preparing a sermon, then, is an art, a science, a discipline, and a relationship. An effective sermon is the child of the union of spiritual dynamics with studious mechanics. The dynamics of sermon preparation arise from the preacher's relationship to the Lord of the text. It is a serious exercise that must be bathed in prayer and enabled by the Holy Spirit from the preacher's very first exposure to a text (see appendix 1).

The purpose of this book, however, is to deal with the mechanics of sermon preparation—the art and science of sculpting a sermon from Scripture.

Definition

Expository preaching is about the Bible and your people. There are many fine definitions of expository preaching.[1] This is my working definition: *Expository preaching is the contemporization of the central proposition of a biblical text that is derived from proper methods of interpretation and declared through effective means of communication to inform minds, instruct hearts, and influence behavior toward godliness.* The components of the definition help us understand the expository task from many dimensions and at many levels.

The "What" of Expository Preaching

The "what" of expository preaching relates to content. Let's go back to the definition to underline the primary content of textual exposition: Expository preaching is *the contemporization of the central proposition of a biblical text* that is derived from proper methods of interpretation and declared through effective means of communication to inform minds, instruct hearts, and influence behavior toward godliness.

Contemporization

Contemporization is the main task of the expository preacher. He takes what was written centuries ago and contemporizes it for present-day audiences. He does not upgrade Scripture. The Bible is already relevant to human issues. The preacher, however, makes God's claims meaningful to the local congregation. Expository preaching contemporizes God's expectations of the audience.

The preacher faces two basic realities: the biblical text of the early century and his context of the present century. Some preachers emphasize the text but make it irrelevant to the modern context. Others emphasize the modern context and are unfaithful to the text.

The exegete studies the meaning of the text of Scripture to find out what God said then. The biblical preacher conducts a creative dialogue and balances the demands of the text and the context to proclaim the significance of the Scripture to us now. He neither negates nor negotiates the realities of the ancient text *or* the modern context. The following is a diagram of the contemporization process.

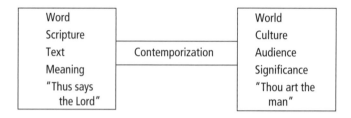

The Central Proposition of a Biblical Text

Throughout the history of expository preaching (and communication theory), most homileticians have been convinced that a single proposition must permeate the entire sermon. Differences exist on where and how one will obtain this central proposition.

In expounding the Bible, there are two possible sources of the pervasive central theme. The preacher may supply it, or the biblical text may supply it. In topical exposition, the preacher chooses the theme. In textual exposition, the text provides the theme. The chart below shows the related features, advantages, and flaws of topical exposition and textual exposition.

Kinds of Biblical Exposition

Subjects	Topical Exposition	Textual Exposition
Features	The preacher chooses the theme and governs the development of the sermon	The text provides the theme and governs the purpose, parameters, and preparation of the sermon
Strengths	• Immediate relevance • Somewhat easier to do	• Long-term relevance • Requires discipline on the preacher's part

Subjects	Topical Exposition	Textual Exposition
Weaknesses	• The text is at the mercy of the preacher • Energy is wasted on choosing the topic of each sermon	• The preacher is at the mercy of the text • Requires discipline on the preacher's part • The preacher may get stuck in exegetical trivia

Exposition is a multidimensional word arising from a Latin root, *expositio (-onis),* a setting forth. Biblical exposition expounds, expresses, and exposes the Bible to an audience and the audience to the Bible. Textual exposition expounds the meaning of a biblical text and its significance to the present context. It expresses a singular proposition that is woven into the sermon. It also exposes the contemporary audience to the truths and claims of God as found in a particular text.

Three Questions to Ask about the Content of Textual Exposition

Have I expounded what the text proposes?
Have I expressed its central proposition in clear and contemporary terms?
Have I exposed the audience to God's truth and claims for learning and obedience?

The "How" of Expository Preaching

The "how" of expository preaching relates to process. Let's look at the definition of expository preaching in terms of the process of our preparation and delivery of the central proposition of the text: Expository preaching is the contemporization of the central proposition of a biblical text that is *derived from proper methods of interpretation and declared through effective means of communication* to inform minds, instruct hearts, and influence behavior toward godliness.

Interpretation

The main criterion for a proper method of interpretation is that there be a demonstrable and reliable connection between the author's and the original audience's understanding of a given text and our interpretation. Step 1 of the Scripture Sculpture process will delineate this process in more detail.

Really, the Bible can be made to say almost anything you may want it to say. The critical question is this: Are you saying what the Bible wanted to say? For example, I heard a fine message on Luke 19:29–40 offer the following truths:

Jesus and the Donkey

I. You are like the donkey (vv. 29–30)
- A. You are tied to someone other than the owner to whom you really belong (v. 30a)
- B. You are still young—no one has sat on you (v. 30b)

II. Jesus commands you to be set free (v. 30c)
- A. He sets you free through his disciples (vv. 31–32)
- B. There will be objections when you are being freed to serve Christ (v. 33)
- C. But he has need of you (v. 34)

III. Are you Christ's donkey? (vv. 35–40)
- A. Is he riding on you?
- B. Are you bringing praise to him?

Can this sermon be preached? It already has been! Is it textually faithful? No! Why? Ask this critical question: Are these points what the author intended to convey and what the original audience understood through this narrative?

This kind of preaching is really "moralistic" preaching. Here are some problems with moralistic preaching:

You do not really need Scripture to come up with such instruction. Any human-interest story will possess moral values. Every culture has parables and accumulated folklore to guide conduct and behavior. What distinguishes scriptural narrative from cultural narrative is the intent of the Holy Spirit as communicated by the human author in a text and as understood by the original audience. Moralism reduces Scripture to good stories alone.

Every text becomes an illustration of a higher moral principle. The text is used as an illustration and not as the source of the point being made. In the "donkey" story, the preacher has decided that the donkey is an illustration of human beings.

Your preaching lacks textual authority. In the donkey story, from where in the text did the preacher get the authority to equate donkeys with human beings? Or suppose when using the text on David and Goliath, the preacher decides that believers will and must face giant-size problems. The illustrative method breaks down since Goliath does not rise again. In reality, giant-size problems have perpetual resurrection power! Thus the illustration lacks textual authority. Unless the sermon demonstrates that the biblical author intended the text to be used in this way, there will be no authority for it.

Such interpretation lacks objective controls. Any preacher can draw any number of illustrations from a given text. There is nothing to control the conclusions he draws. Why five rather than three points or two rather than seven points?

The central proposition of your sermon is not discernibly related to or derived from the central proposition of the text. The interpretation of the preacher (and therefore the force of the sermon) becomes arbitrary. The people will begin to see sermons as the preacher's whimsical use of a given text.

Proper methods of interpretation must form the backbone of the sermon. The preacher is first an exegete of Scripture before he is an expositor of Scripture.

Communication

If proper methods of interpretation relate to the author's and the original audience's understanding of the text, then effective communication relates to the connection between the preacher's and present audience's understanding of a text.

For instance, a friend and I did a seminar on planning for local church leaders in the Far East. My friend taught the first session on why we should plan. His first major point: We should plan because God plans. God planned creation, redemption, and the kingdom. Therefore, we must plan as well.

The problem with that presentation was that it did not take into account the audience's understanding of the truth. Their worldview, premises, values, and beliefs all interfered with their understanding of my friend's point. Unfortunately, the conclusion they drew after considering divine planning was the opposite of my friend's point. They had concluded: If God plans, we don't have to plan!

For our communication to be effective, we must understand the worldview, reasoning process, and culture of the audience. And then, using analogies and illustrations, appropriate style and delivery, and relevant application we will claim their obedience. We will consider some of these aspects in step 6 of the Scripture Sculpture process.

The "Why" of Expository Preaching

The "why" of expository preaching relates to purpose. What is the purpose of our preparation and delivery of an expository sermon? Let's go back to our working definition: Expository preaching is the contemporization of the central proposition of a biblical text that is derived from proper methods of interpretation and declared through effective means of communication *to inform minds, instruct hearts, and influence behavior toward godliness.* The why of expository preaching primarily deals with intellectual, affective, and volitional components of Christian experience.

Inform the Mind

As a result of their exposure to the sermon, our hearers must *know* and *understand* something—God's truth. Normally, this knowledge relates to the central proposition of the sermon. If they do not know more of what God says and expects of them as a result of our preaching, we are not necessary. The Lord Jesus added loving God with our minds to his version of the greatest commandment (see Matt. 22:36–37).

Instruct the Heart

Not all human decisions are made rationally. Emotional factors play a big part in serious decisions. We must appeal not only to the emotions, however. The heart must be instructed while the mind is being informed. It is possible and necessary to address the seat of all emotions—the heart—through expository preaching. The preacher must leave his audience enthusiastic about obeying God. If the Word has instructed the hearts of our audience, we can be confident that these feelings are neither superficial nor artificial. As a result of our preaching, our audience must both *feel* and *will* something—the necessity of personal obedience to God's truth.

Influence Behavior

The practical test of good preaching is the fruit that it bears in life. The Bible was given for behavioral change (2 Tim. 3:16–17). Works must follow faith (cf. the Book of James). As a result of our preaching, our audience will *do* something. They will obey. Godliness must result in their lives. That is, the pulpit is not just for disseminating more information, it is the platform from which our hearers are motivated to godliness by example and exposition. They must know what God expects and how they may obey God's mandates from any text of Scripture. Preaching must result in godliness.

I made a commitment to my people in New Delhi. I said to them, "When I stop giving you something more to know, something more to feel, and something more to do as a result of our time together around God's Word, it will be time to turn off the lights at the church."

From Text to Sermon

Here are the seven steps from text to sermon in the process of sculpting Scripture. You should memorize these steps.

The Seven-Step Scripture Sculpture Process

7. Preach the Sermon	"Flesh"
6. Structure the Sermon	"Skeleton"
5. The Central Proposition of the Sermon	"Heart"
4. The Purpose Bridge	"Brain"
3. The Central Proposition of the Text	"Heart"
2. Structure the Text	"Skeleton"
1. Study the Text	"Flesh"

On the right side of the chart, I have listed the parts of a living sculpture that we attempt to create with each sermon.

1. *Study the text.* By studying the details of a text, we acquire the "flesh" of the text.
2. *Structure the text.* In structuring the text, we have the skeletal makeup of this text. The flesh and the skeleton form the textual raw materials for the sculpting process.
3. *The central proposition of the text.* From the skeleton, we discern the central proposition of the text, the "heart" of its meaning.
4. *The purpose bridge.* From the heart of the text we develop a purpose for our audience. This sermonic purpose is the "brain" by which the sermon is finally designed and preached.
5. *The central proposition of the sermon.* The brain will yield the direction and the form of the heart of the sermon.
6. *Structure the sermon.* The sermon will now form its own image and outline. The skeleton of the message will be evident.
7. *Preach the sermon.* Finally, we will fill in the details for the flesh as we finish sculpting a specialized, tailor-made sermon for our particular audience.

Another way of diagramming the seven steps:

From Text to Sermon

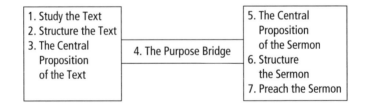

After coming up with this sermon preparation system, I saw an easy way to remember the seven steps. Below are some tips to help you remember this sequence.

- Step 3 (text side) and step 5 (sermon side) are parallel, dealing with the heart or central proposition.

- Step 2 (text side) and step 6 (sermon side) both deal with skeleton or structure.
- Step 1 (text side) and step 7 (sermon side) deal with the flesh or basic blocks.
- Step 4 is the bridge or brain that helps us make a transition from the text to the sermon.

Numbering or lettering the steps gives us an easy pattern to remember: 1 2 3 4 3 2 1 or A B C D C B A. By the way, this kind of parallelism is also found in the Hebrew Bible and is known as a chiastic construction. The external similarity with the Bible does not make this sermon preparation system inspired and inerrant. This system will, however, enable you, an errant human being, to compose an inspiring sermon.

Below is a summary description of each step of sculpting a sermon. These steps serve as an overview of the rest of the manual.

Step 1: Studying the Text—The Flesh of the Text

Step 1 introduces the student to the fundamental process of studying a text. It provides several keys to finding the meaning of the text. It lays down the groundwork for serious study in accurately "seeing" and "seeking" what the Bible desires to communicate to all people.

Step 2: Structuring the Text—The Skeleton of the Text

An essential step in the sculpturing process is understanding how the biblical author put the text together. In this way, we are able not only to preach what the author said but even emphasize how he said it. Step 2 gives clues on how to find the structure of a text so that you can summarize the teaching of each section of the text.

Step 3: The Central Proposition of the Text—The Heart of the Text

As the heart is to the human, so the central proposition is to the text (and later to the sermon). Step 3 will help you discover the dominant teaching of the text, what the text proposes, under two headings:

The Theme: What is the author talking about?

The Thrust: What is the author saying about what he is talking about?

Everything in the text is woven around the single major theme. When the theme/thrust is found, one can confidently expound the text under the authority of God.

Step 4: The Purpose of the Sermon—The Brain of the Sermon

Step 4 is critical to making expository preaching relevant to the audience. The purpose is the brain of the sermon, the key link from text to sermon. You will learn to clearly articulate the purpose of the sermon in relation to your audience.

Step 5: The Central Proposition of the Sermon—The Heart of the Sermon

Just as the text has a singular theme/thrust, your sermon must have a singular theme/thrust. The central proposition of your sermon will contain the twin "theme and thrust" emphasis. Here the biblical proposition (step 3) is channeled through the purpose (step 4) and contemporized to be understood and obeyed by the audience.

Step 6: Structuring the Sermon—The Skeleton of the Sermon

In this step you will consider the basic ways of developing a sermon with unity, order, and progress. Sample forms of development that effect comprehension and elicit obedience will be proposed.

Step 7: Preaching the Sermon—The Flesh of the Sermon

You can increase the impact of your sermon through illustrations, proper word usage, and your physical delivery. A comprehensive questionnaire to evaluate your messages and those of others is included in appendix 12. You will also be advised to write out the sermon as best and as much as you can before preaching it.

You are in the right place in this manual if:

- you are just about to get into expository preaching
- you want to be clear about how to draw material from a text for your sermons

THE
SCRIPTURE SCULPTURE
PROCESS

1

STUDY THE TEXT

The "Flesh" of the Text

Step 7: Preach the Sermon
Step 6: Structure the Sermon
Step 5: The Central Proposition of the Sermon
Step 4: The Purpose Bridge
Step 3: The Central Proposition of the Text
Step 2: Structure the Text
Step 1: Study the Text

Studying the biblical text is step 1 of the sermon-preparation process.* Normally in a pulpit ministry that pursues expository preaching, no energy or time is wasted on choosing a passage to preach. You simply preach the next segment of the biblical portion that you are presently preaching. (Some considerations for choosing relevant texts are found in appendix 3.)

---

* If you are familiar with systematic and methodical study of a biblical text, you may proceed to step 2. I recommend, however, that you review step 1 as a refresher course in basic Bible study methods.

The expository preaching of a text assumes that you will study a passage intelligently, intentionally, and interactively. You study a text intelligently because you love God with your whole being, which includes your mind. You study a text intentionally since you want to recover the express purpose that God has for you and your people in that text. And you will find God calling for your own submission and change as you interact with the text.

There are two facets of such study.[1]

Step 1

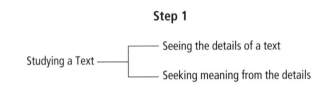

Seeing: Your study of the text will deal with all the details you can "see" in the text.

Seeking: Your conclusions from the study of the text will result from the questions you ask of the details of a given passage and your answers to those questions.

Seeing the Details of a Text

To see the text is to observe what information God has put in a biblical passage. *All* the details of a text are important, because we believe in the full inspiration of Scripture. Make all possible observations from a text. You can and will throw out inappropriate observations later.

What should you observe? You should observe the words and the relationships between the words.

Observe Words

Take note of *key* words in the text. Words determine the content of your text and influence your construction of its meaning. I find it

helpful to deal with one verse on one sheet of paper. Write the whole
verse at the top of the page and underline the key words. Key words
that you should study are long words, unusual words, repeated words.

Words to Observe

- Long words
- Unusual words
- Repeated words

Action Step

Open your Bible to Psalm 117. Write out verse 1 at the top of one sheet of paper
and underline its key words. Do the same with verse 2 on a second page. You will
study words such as *praise, nations, lovingkindness, truth, everlasting.*

Observe Relationships

Some kinds of relationships you will observe are:

- Grammatical relationships: How are words put together in the
  text? Basic observations would include relationships between
  tenses (past, present, future), *number* (singular, plural), and
  gender (masculine, feminine, neuter).
- Logical relationships: How are thoughts put together in the
  text? How does the author build a case or argument for his
  point?
- Chronological and/or geographical relationships: What are the
  times and places that are involved in the text?
- Psychological relationships: Are there any psychological
  aspects to this text that are stated or implied in the words?
- Contextual relationships: In what context does this text occur?
  You will need to take immediate and wider contexts into
  account:
  —The context of the Bible
  —The context of the book
  —The context of the text

- Relationships in genre: Relationships in genre have to do with the kind of biblical literature in which a passage is found. Here are some kinds of literature that are found in the Bible.

  —Teaching: didactic or discourse material like Jesus' sermons or the Epistles

  —Narratives: narration of historical events

  —Poetry: Psalms, Proverbs, Song of Solomon, and others

  —Parables: primarily in the parables of Christ

  —Miracles: primarily found in three periods of biblical history—Moses and Aaron, Elijah and Elisha, the Lord and the apostles

  —Prophetic: futuristic books like sections of Daniel, Ezekiel, Revelation, and also the major and minor prophets of the Old Testament

Seeking Meaning from the Details of a Passage

While *seeing* has to do with the details of a passage, *seeking* has to do with the meaning of those details. There is no point in seeing parts and not seeking the whole. Seeking meaning deals with interpreting the observations, and seeing and seeking are most often and best done simultaneously. Interpretation is basically asking questions of your observations and answering them.

Asking Questions

You must ask questions. In asking questions lies the art of discovery in any discipline. A simple difference between advanced and beginning students is the ability to ask many good questions. Ask questions of the words. Ask questions of the relationships between the words you have marked as important in understanding a text.

Seeing Details	Seeking Meaning
• Words	• Questions for Words
• Relationships	• Questions for Relationships

Questions for Words

Ask what the words mean today. Look them up in an English or vernacular dictionary. A good dictionary will not only tell you what a word means now but also what it meant at the time of your translation (e.g., 1611, King James Version). The meaning of many words has changed over the years. For example, in the new English versions of the Bible, the Third Person of the Trinity is the Holy *Spirit* (Gk. *pneuma,* Matt. 28:19), and the disciples are afraid of a *ghost* (Gk. *phantasma,* Matt. 14:26). In the older versions, the Third Person of the Trinity is consistently referred to as the Holy *Ghost* while the disciples are afraid of a *spirit!*

Ask what the words meant at the time they were written. Look up the words in a Bible dictionary or Bible encyclopedia.

Ask how the Bible or the author used these words elsewhere and how other biblical authors used them. There are several ways to find these answers. The marginal references in your Bible will guide you to key usages of the word elsewhere. Also, a concordance will help immensely. You should ask these same questions of key phrases and repeated statements in your text.

Questions for Relationships

The English language is often peculiar. For example, *vegetarians* eat vegetables, but *humanitarians* do not eat humans! If you are able to handle the vocabulary and inconsistencies of English, no language will be a challenge for you.

Relationships between words, for the most part, have to do with grammar. Grammar helps us discern the point of a sentence and eventually groups of related sentences. During my childhood, I learned how to use grammar without knowing how it "works." I have found that grammar is like automobile mechanics. I drive a car without knowing how it works. And I get stuck when the car breaks down! It used to be that when my English broke down I did not know how to fix it, either. Eventually, English grammar became clearer to me. For those like me, I have included an introduction to English grammar in appendix 4 of this manual. Understanding English grammar will also help you analyze a biblical text in other languages—especially if you are learning other languages through English.

We ask questions of the same relationships that we observed under seeing the details of a text: grammatical, logical, chronological, and other relationships.

Grammatical Relationships

If you observe the details of Matthew 16:18, you will see that the Lord Jesus uses the future *tense:* "I *will* build My church" (emphasis mine). In Matthew 28:19 he uses the word *name* in the singular when referring to the three persons of the Trinity. Note the use of the definite article in Ephesians 4:13: "unity of *the* faith" (emphasis mine). If you use Greek in your study, you will notice the neuter gender, as in John 10:30: "I and the Father are *one*" (emphasis mine).

Turn to appendix 2 for the answer to an important question I am asked at seminars on preaching: "Is it possible to preach and preach effectively without knowing the original languages of the Bible?"

Logical Relationships

Logical relationships help us understand the case, the point, or the argument the author is making. In the following list of illustrations from Scripture, note the words I have put in italics. Words like these help us determine the relationship between sets of words. You would not have studied these as key words. These are usually short words that significantly influence the meaning of the details.

- Cause and effect: "We love, *because* He first loved us" (1 John 4:19).
- Reason: "*If then* [meaning "since"] you have been raised up with Christ, keep seeking the things above" (Col. 3:1).

- Result: Speaking about elders who faithfully shepherd the flock of God, Peter writes: "And *when* the Chief Shepherd appears, you will receive the unfading crown of glory" (1 Peter 5:4). The *result* of faithful shepherding is the reward the Chief Shepherd brings.

    Or, the practical importance of the doctrine of the rapture for present comfort is built on the reason or result word *therefore* in 1 Thessalonians 4:18 (cf. 1 Thess. 4:13–18).

- Contrast: Ephesians 2 speaks of our former spiritual existence (vv. 1–3); "*But* God . . ." (v. 4) *contrasts* our present spiritual existence with our former one, hinging on the word *but*.

- Comparisons: "Greater is He who is in you *than* he who is in the world" (1 John 4:4). The two who vie for human allegiance are *compared*.

- Condition: 2 Chronicles 7:14: "*If* my people . . . *then* . . ." The *condition* for God's response is our calling on his name.

- Purpose: Ephesians 4:12 gives the *purpose* for which God gave special leaders to the church, "*for* the equipping of . . ."

Again, all of these logical relationships are set forth by means of words and progressions of words.

Chronological and/or Geographical Relationships

These relationships are especially helpful in structuring (descriptive outlining) narrative literature such as historical material and miracle events. Two examples follow.

The Book of Acts is given in chronological and geographical sequence. This sequence is introduced in Acts 1:8.

- Jerusalem (1:1–8:3). The spread of the Christian faith in Jerusalem.

- Samaria (8:4–12:25). Also notice here the *effect* of scattering the Christians that was *caused* by persecution. When you interpret the text, you see this as a literary device used by Luke to tell us about the sovereign hand of God in evangelism.

- The remotest part of the earth (13:1–28:31).

In Luke 17:11–19 the miracle of the ten lepers can be traced in a similar manner.

- Jesus deals with the *ten* who were in need and were healed (vv. 11–14).
- The narrative then focuses on the *one* who returned to say thanks (vv. 15–19).

The Book of Jonah lends itself easily to a chronological and geographical study.

- Jonah *in* Israel ministering (1:1–2)
- Jonah *on* the boat fleeing to Tarshish (1:3–14)
- Jonah *in* the fish praying (1:15–2:10)
- Jonah *at* Nineveh preaching (3:1–10)
- Jonah *under* a shelter (outside Nineveh) pouting (4:1–11)

Psychological Relationships

Observing psychological relationships may seem like a hazardous way of interpreting texts since the term *psychological* may imply arbitrary subjectivity. But an attempt to understand psychological issues is necessary in discerning the meaning of distinctive literature such as parables, miracles, and other material that relate to human relationships. For example, we recognize the tender relationship of the shepherd and sheep (Psalm 23; John 10). Seeing how a shepherd feels about his sheep will help us understand the feeling of the divine Shepherd toward his sheep.

Also, to really understand the miracle of the healing of the ten lepers, we need to discern some of the tensions between Jews and Samaritans and why it was significant that a foreigner should give thanks to Jesus when his own people didn't. Luke clearly contrasts these two sets of people in a *psychologically* significant way with regard to their gratitude toward Jesus. Jesus dealt with the ten who needed healing (Luke 17:11–14), but nine took healing for granted. The narrative points to the one who gave thanks even though he was a foreigner (Luke 17:15–19).

By observing the details that the writers give concerning the psychological aspects of the human relationships portrayed in the miracles, we gain a deeper understanding of the Scripture. This is not an exercise in psychologizing Scripture but in asking if the text gives us psychological material to take into account, to get to the author's meaning.

Contextual Relationships

Any passage is surrounded by the literary context of the whole and parts of Scripture.

The Bible context. The entire Bible is one grand story. It is God's view of history—*his story.* The origin of the universe and man, the making of God's chosen people in the Old Testament, the first coming of the Lord Jesus Christ, the revelation of the mystery that all peoples can be equal heirs to God's salvation in Christ Jesus, and the final events of our time-space world revolve around Christ Jesus as the divine Redeemer of humanity. The contents of the entire Bible fit into this story from the creation of the earth to the creation of the new earth.

Many of God's servants have not seen the whole picture. And without seeing the whole picture, they pick a verse out of Genesis or Isaiah or Matthew and radiate good thoughts about it. They are probably not being unbiblical, but it is important to ask if they are saying what the text is saying. They must take into account the total context of Scripture: the historical context in the biblical progression of history, the biblical context, the cultural context, and the theological context.

When considering the biblical or literary context, a verse from the Pentateuchal narratives will be interpreted with narrative features in mind, and the Psalms will be better understood with poetry in mind. For more advanced students, other issues that must be taken into account in preaching narrative are summarized in appendix 6. It is sufficient to note that the Bible is written in many literary styles, and we ought to interpret passages in keeping with the intention, form, and style of the authors.

The cultural context must also be considered. For example, Amos's audience was different from Paul's audience, not only theologically but culturally.

When viewed from a theological context, a passage that is contained in the precross legal texts of the Old Testament cannot be treated in the same interpretive way as the ethical instruction lists (sometimes called housetable texts) found in a Pauline epistle.

It is necessary, therefore, to get a panoramic view of the entire biblical story from Genesis to Revelation. *Hint:* If you cannot think through the story of the Bible, read a survey of the Bible. Introductory works like *Willmington's Bible Handbook* (Willmington, Wheaton: Tyndale, 1997) or *Talk thru the Bible* (Wilkinson and Boa, Nashville: Nelson, 1983) will help immensely.

The context of the book. Every book in the Bible was written by an intelligent author under the supervision of the Holy Spirit. Each book was purposely written in a particular way. Its purpose influenced its contents. So observe the contents of the book to understand its purpose. This purpose will in turn help you interpret it before you expound it.

For illustration, take a book like Job. Read the book two or three times. Simply speaking, it is the story of a righteous rich man named Job who went through immense suffering. Three friends, in three conferences with Job, try to help him understand his suffering, but each time they point to wrong causes. A fourth friend comes nearer to the truth, but the ultimate response to Job's existential and theological question comes through a dynamic revelation of the word and works of Almighty God.

As you study the book, you will notice the following divisions within the narrative (numbers refer to chapters):

Introduction: Job's Distress 1–2
First Conference 3–14
Second Conference 15–21
Third Conference 22–31
Elihu's Speeches 32–37
God's Response 38–41
Conclusion: Job's Deliverance 41

After studying the book with these divisions in mind, when you come to a favorite verse such as, "And as for me, I know that my

Redeemer lives," you can immediately place the verse in Job's reply in the second round of speeches (19:25). The verse is an expression of vital hope in the context of hopeless despair and is not primarily an Easter text. It is a reply to specific comments made by Bildad concerning the postdeath fate of the wicked. Suddenly then, hope and confidence in the living God are evident in the most serious suffering.

Knowing the entire book helps you grapple with the serious issue of what the author meant by his writings. To recover the author's intention is the goal of all interpretation.

Hint: Some of the best resources in studying the contents and purpose of a given book are study and reference Bibles. They often have helpful comments at the beginning of each book. The commentators' ideas may differ a little in their perceptions of the author's purpose and outline. Thus they will serve as added input for your consideration in arriving at the author's purpose and structure. It is best to study the book for yourself first, however, and then compare your ideas to those of other scholars. This process will be easier with some biblical books than others. But do not give up. The biblical preacher must have a working knowledge of the book in which his text appears.

The context of the text. The basic unit of Bible study is not the verse or the sentence but the paragraph. I have already mentioned that expository preaching saves time and energy when deciding what to preach each Sunday. As you do your book study, you will notice that the text is divided into paragraphs. Normally, you can preach a paragraph each time.

The context of the text becomes crucial when an author is building points on the points of a previous passage. Further, it may not be possible to finish an entire paragraph in one sermon. You may be able to preach only the first and the second points of the text. In this case, you must study the preceding verses and sometimes the succeeding contexts in preparation for a sermon.

To illustrate the importance of the context of the text in helping you understand its meaning, go to the Book of 1 Peter. In 2:13 the main issue is submission. If we had turned directly to the responsibilities of the husband in 3:7, we probably would not have understood the force in that text of the word *likewise* for husbands. Peter has already spoken about submission, even when treated unjustly, to government authorities and to other masters. If we miss out on the force of the total context on submission, then in our preaching to husbands we will not touch on one of the key issues in domestic relationships—mutual submission, respect, and loyalty between husband and wife. Perhaps "husband preachers" would like not to see that word!

Relationships in Genre

Here we emphasize what has already been intimated about the different kinds of literature found in the Bible. Our interpretive approach to a text will be influenced by the style in which it is written. For instance, we look at a text written in a narrative style differently than we would an epistle.

Do not make all the details of a narrative text carry applicational value to your audience. The historical details can be mentioned and will add interest to the presentation, but not all of them can be directly applied to our lives today. To illustrate, we go back to the Book of Jonah—a typical narrative of a historical event. When it comes to preaching the story of Jonah, we do not propose that we should not get into boats. Instead, we may propose a truth such as no place is outside God's pursuit when we are running from him. The point of the early Jonah narrative is not the proper means of transportation but the necessity of obedience to the known will of God. The details of the narrative describe the historical event and help us arrive at the theological truth uniquely portrayed in the passage.

Another example is that of Paul. Even though he walked around in sandals in Asia Minor and got bitten by snakes, we cannot preach that Christians should do the same. We can preach, however, that dangers will be encountered in pioneering evangelism in difficult areas.

These kinds of hermeneutical adjustments for homiletical application are almost intuited by the interpreter/preacher.

The homiletical and applicational adjustments are sometimes referred to as "principilization"—the abstracting of a theological principle from a text for applicational impact. In steps 3 to 5 of the Scripture Sculpture process, I will show how this may be done safely and precisely. I must alert you, however, to some dangers in such principilization. Your principle must be drawn from the text rather than imposed on the text. It must relate to the structure and details of the text. I will deal with this part of the process later. (A more technical treatment of principilization is found in appendix 5.)

Genre is also a factor when interpreting and preaching parables. Parables usually have one major emphasis that cannot be ignored. One cannot preach a parable applicationally in all its details. The same is true of the miracles of our Lord. Still another kind of literature is the poetry of Psalms and Job. Prophetic literature is unique. When we interpret this genre, we must take its prophetic nature into account. For example, when we compare the word *weeks* in Daniel 9:24 and Daniel 10:2, we conclude that the "weeks" are of different lengths. Four hundred and ninety days is too short a time to accomplish the prophecy of Daniel 9:24–27, and twenty-one years is too long for Daniel to fast and survive (10:3).

Summary of Questions to Ask

An easy way to remember the kinds of questions that the preacher needs to ask of a text is to divide them into four categories:

1. Background questions
2. Fact questions
3. Meaning questions
4. Application questions

- *Background questions:* For example, how does the historical background of Colossians affect the content of Paul's writing?
- *Fact questions:* How does Paul describe himself in Colossians 1:1–2?
- *Meaning questions:* Why does Paul describe himself in this way? What does it mean to be raised to new life in Christ (Col. 2:12)?
- *Application questions:* How can we set our minds on things above (Col. 3:2)?

Answering Questions

Here we come to the hard work of interpretation. In answering the questions, we ought to be careful that we do not manipulate the text in our attempts to master it. The plain, natural interpretation of Scripture (some call it "literal," and others call it "grammatical-historical interpretation") is what the expositor is after. Basically, interpreting Scripture *on its own terms* is what is most important in understanding its meaning.

At this juncture of preparation you may bring in whatever resources for Bible study that you have access to. If you do not know the original languages, I suggest that you consider obtaining a good study Bible, a concordance for the version you own, one commentary series (a one-volume consolidated commentary will be a good start), and a good Bible dictionary. These are bare necessities. Read these for their input into your questions and answers. Remember that these are only aids to your preparation. Do not touch them until you have come to this stage of your sermon preparation. They will influence your questions and conclusions if you consult them before this time, and this will hinder the preparation process by which the text becomes a part of your very being.

Analyzing Answers

Robert Traina, in his *Methodical Bible Study,*[2] speaks of three dangers in interpreting Scripture:

- *Misinterpretation:* assigning the wrong meaning to a passage
- *Subinterpretation:* the failure to ascertain the full meaning of a passage
- *Superinterpretation:* attributing more significance to a passage than is actually implicit in it

Much ink has flowed on how to interpret a passage. But on the popular level, you will analyze your answers with the following tests:

- *The test of authenticity.* Can you make a good case that your interpretation is authentic? That is, is your interpretation true to what the author meant when writing these words?

- *The test of unity.* Is there unity of meaning between the terms, affirmations, and interpretation of the text? Is there a contradiction or discrepancy in your interpretation? For example, I once heard a sermon on 1 John in which *brother* meant Christian in the first half and non-Christian in the second half of the sermon.

- *The test of consistency.* Is your interpretation consistent with the rest of the chapter, book, and the entire Bible? Can you explain an apparent difficulty? For example, how do you explain Paul's giving Timothy permission to eat all meats in comparison with Old Testament prohibitions?

- *The test of simplicity.* Is your interpretation simple or contrived? Plain or mystical? Easily stated and understood or heavily supported by allusions and concoctions of arguments?

- *The test of honesty.* Have you been careful not to read yours or others' (e.g., your Bible teacher's or your denomination's) prejudgments and preconceptions into the text?

Please note: Since our interpretations are not infallible, we must always leave open the possibility for change as new evidence and/or questions are brought to bear on the interpretation.

Testing your Interpretation of a Biblical Passage

1. Authenticity
2. Unity
3. Consistency
4. Simplicity
5. Honesty

Applying Answers

Preaching does not only have to do with transferring information; it has to do with transferring information that transforms people. What we preach ought to change lives. It ought to challenge men and women to apply the truth of the Bible in the very structure of their lives. The preacher's responsibility is to delineate not only principles for application but pointers for application. We cannot leave it to the audience to find ways and means to creatively apply Scripture.

First, we must and will apply Scripture in our own lives. Then we will show people how to integrate biblical truth into their lives. At this stage of the sermon-preparation process, we are already thinking of what the Bible is saying to our people based on what the Bible means. What is the significance of the text under study for modern daily life?

Before going into a methodology for application, here is a fine definition of application from Roy B. Zuck.

> Application in biblical exposition (preaching or teaching) may be defined as the process of communicating the present-day relevance of a biblical text, specifying how that relevance may be translated into action, and inviting and urging the hearers to make that transference.[3]

Application may be *content* oriented, relating to what the hearers should believe or value, or it may be *conduct* oriented, relating to what they should do or obey. Often these two orientations in application are intermingled simply because people will often do only what they value.

To make proper application you must ask the following rigorous questions.

- What is the application (present-day relevance) of the text?
- What kind of application should you draw from the text? Content, conduct, or conduct based on content?
- Is my application really based on this text? Does it have the authority and authenticity of the text behind it?
- What will convince my audience that this is the application from the text?
- How can I be sure that the people will understand the application of the text? That is, we cannot take it for granted that

they have understood the application. Application is not automatic. Actually, people are not prone to apply truths to themselves. They would rather apply them to someone else!

As you study the text, you will be looking for personal and preaching application points. And often you will begin to apply these even before your sermon takes shape. Record the applications you think arise from a text. You will later dispense with the applications that do not carry textual authority or have textual warranty (step 3) and that will not fit your purpose (step 4). Eugene Lowry suggests an interesting integration. "Wear the hats of scholar and homiletician *throughout* the sermon preparation process."[4]

Action Step

Let's apply the first step of the Scripture Sculpture process, "Study the Text," to a sample text from the epistles, Ephesians 6:10–12. Check the progress of each phase of this first step as you work through this text.

Use one sheet of paper per verse. Write it out in full:

[10]Finally, be strong in the Lord, and in the strength of His might.

[11]Put on the whole armor of God, that you may be able to stand firm against the schemes of the devil.

[12]For our struggle is not against flesh and blood, but against the rulers, against the powers, against the world forces of this darkness, against the spiritual forces of wickedness in heavenly places.

Seeing the Details

Observe Words

Study their meanings in dictionaries, Bible dictionaries, or encyclopedias, and study their usage from entries in concordances and marginal references.

In this text you would observe words such as: *strong, armor, schemes, struggle, rulers, powers, forces.*

Observe Relationships

Here you would observe relationships, such as "finally," "in the Lord," "strength of His might," "schemes of the devil," "flesh and blood," and different aspects of the nonhuman foes in verse 12.

Seeking Meaning

Ask Questions

Why does Paul say "Finally" in verse 10? Is it possible to be strong without the Lord? Or is it necessary because of the kind of supernatural opposition he describes in verse 12 that we need supernatural strength? Also, why the *full* armor of God?

Answer Questions

Finally could mean "of utmost importance" and could refer to the entire epistle, or it could refer back to the content of chapters 4–6. The *full* armor of God is recommended because it is necessary to protect our vulnerable areas of life from Satan's comprehensive attack.

Analyze Answers

Using the tests detailed above, analyze your answers. Also, check commentaries on what other men of God have to say on this text. For instance, one commentator writes, "The form of the Greek imperative *put on* indicates that believers are responsible for putting on God's (not their) full armor . . . with all urgency."[5]

Apply Answers

Where are the "urgent" areas of Satan's attack and our response to him? Think through some contemporary ways in which the struggle against Satan continues. Also, write down ways in which we can stand strong in the Lord and how you and your people can apply them.

Step 1: Study the Text (An Outline of Step 1)

I. Seeing
   A. Observe Words
      1. Long words
      2. Unusual words
      3. Repeated words
   B. Observe Relationships
      1. Grammatical relationships
      2. Logical relationships
      3. Chronological and/or geographical relationships
      4. Psychological relationships
      5. Contextual relationships
         a. The context of the Bible
         b. The context of the book

       c. The context of the text

     6. Relationships in genre

       a. Teaching

       b. Narratives

       c. Poetry

       d. Parables

       e. Miracles

       f. Prophecy

II. Seeking

  A. Asking Questions

    1. Questions for words

      a. What do these words mean now?

      b. What did these words mean at the time they were written?

      c. How have the Bible, the author, and authors used these words elsewhere?

    2. Questions for relationships

      a. Grammatical relationships

       (1) Tense

       (2) Number

       (3) Gender

      b. Logical relationships

       (1) Cause and effect

       (2) Reason

       (3) Result

       (4) Contrast

       (5) Comparisons

       (6) Conditions

       (7) Purpose

      c. Chronological and/or geographical relationships

      d. Psychological relationships

      e. Contextual relationships

       (1) The Bible context

        (a) The historical context

        (b) The biblical or literary context

        (c) The cultural context

        (d) The theological context

       (2) The context of the book

       (3) The context of the text

      f. Relationships in genre

    3. Summary: kinds of questions

      a. Background questions
      b. Fact questions
      c. Meaning questions
      d. Application questions
  B. Answering Questions
  C. Analyzing Answers: "Five Tests"
    1. Authenticity
    2. Unity
    3. Consistency
    4. Simplicity
    5. Honesty
  D. Applying Answers
    1. What kind of application?
    2. What is the application?
    3. What is the legitimate basis of the application?
    4. How can I leave the audience sure that the authority of the text is the basis for this application?

2

STRUCTURE THE TEXT

The "Skeleton" of the Text

Step 7: Preach the Sermon
Step 6: Structure the Sermon
Step 5: The Central Proposition of the Sermon
Step 4: The Purpose Bridge
Step 3: The Central Proposition of the Text
Step 2: Structure the Text
Step 1: Study the Text

Step 2 builds on your study of the text (step 1). An essential step in the Scripture Sculpture process is to understand *how* the biblical author put the text together. In this way, not only can we preach what the author says, but we even emphasize how he said it. Step 2 gives clues on how to find the structure of a text with a view to summarizing the teaching of each section of the passage.

Step 2 is climbed by structuring and summarizing the sections of the text.

Step 2

Structuring the sections of the text
Summarizing the sections of the text

Structuring the Sections of the Text

We find the structure of a text with the help of two kinds of structure indicators: grammatical keys and content cues.

Grammatical Keys

Grammatical keys are usually little words or parts of words wielding a disproportionately large influence on the composition of a text. These little words are skipped over too often but form the very basis of the argument and emphasis of the author. You may recall my comments in step 1 on "logical relationships" between words and phrases (see pages 38–39).

Here is an example of a critical, little word at work. Take the short sentence: "John came here for he was hungry." The word *for* has only three letters but is crucial in understanding the argument of the sentence. *For* gives the reason for John's coming. The same thought could be expressed by another small word: "I came here *as* I was hungry." *As* here again gives the reason for my coming.

Biblical literature has many such little words and parts of words that are loaded with power. Some of these dynamic little words, with the general meanings that they carry, are given below.

Action Step

Turn to Ezra 7:10. The NASB reads:

For Ezra had set his heart to study the law of the LORD, and to practice it, and to teach His statues and ordinances in Israel.

Go through step 1 on this text, marking the longer, unusual, and repeated words for study and meditation.

In step 2 you will discover the structure of the text. You will identify the author's main point(s) and subpoints.

In Ezra 7:10 notice the twofold repetition of the connecting word *and* relating three phrases:

"Ezra had set his heart
to study the law of the LORD,
and
to practice it
and
to teach"

The verse then naturally divides into three parts. You can confidently assert this threefold division as arising from the text rather than a division imposed on the verse. There is a third *and* between *statutes* and *ordinances.* You will have to decide whether to give this *and* the same weight as earlier *ands.* You will not do so, because the third *and* simply connects two words. The earlier *ands* connect phrases within the verse, and each is followed by an infinitive "to." I show aspects of this structure below.

If you eventually structure this verse for preaching, the *body* of your sermon will not usually contain more than three points (a sermon may have fewer or more points— we will come to that matter later). That is, the portion of your sermon that directly deals with this verse will and should have only three points.

Below and on the next page is a simple but important chart to use for future reference. As you come across these little words, consult this chart for the possible range of interpretations of those words. For example, if you come across the word *for,* your interpretation of that portion will hinge around cause or reason or result or purpose.

Here is a clue for those who cannot use the original languages of the Bible: A rather reliable structural marker is the verse divisions of a text. While verse, paragraph, and chapter divisions are not inspired, they are reliable indicators of thought and structure that scholarly translators have determined as they have studied each text. Even punctuation marks in verses are indicators of structure. So be sure to notice periods (full stops), colons, semicolons, commas, and exclamation points, and all other punctuation.

Grammatical Keys Indicating Structure

Meaning	*Little Words as Structure Indicators*
Cause	for, because, since, as
Reason	for, because, since, as, that

Meaning	Little Words as Structure Indicators
Result	that, so that, so, which, for
Purpose	in order that, which, to, unto, until, towards, for
Means	by, from, through, out of, in
Time	until, till, to, when, whenever, from, through, of, in, by, according to, against, with, concerning, out of
Place	where, wherever, from, in, through, into, upon, with, concerning, till
Manner	just as, just, as, with, to

Note: Other "little words" will emerge in your study that are not included here. You may classify their meaning according to context and good sense. Also see the illustration of structuring the text of Ephesians 6:10–12 at the end of this chapter.

Content Cues

Sometimes structure is not indicated by grammar. Instead, the structure of a text can be discerned by:

- content changes
- introduction of a new subject
- repetition
- change in the form of statement, and so on

An example of a change in the form of statement is when the author is making declarations and suddenly changes into a command or imperative mood. You should take that change into account as you discern the structure of the text.

Four Steps for Structuring Text

The following four steps will help you structure the sections of the text:

- *Identify* all possible grammatical or content markers of structure.
- *Separate* major markers from minor markers. Major markers carry more weight in structuring the text than the minor markers.

- *Understand* the meaning or the force of the more major markers.
- *Outline* the text according to the relative importance of the markers.

This structuring phase attempts to separate the more important markers from the less important markers. Just as bodies have big bones and little bones to connect and separate various parts from others, so biblical texts (and all good writing) feature big bones and little bones. You will use your interpretive judgments along with those of others to understand the major and minor divisions of your text. If we think of our text as made up of big bones and little bones, here is how the four steps would look:

Big Bones vs. Small Bones (Understanding Structure)

- Identify all the bones.
- Separate big bones from little bones.
- Understand the meaning or the force of the big bones.
- Lay out the bones according to their importance.

How do we apply these four steps to a text? Here I describe them and then illustrate them from Scripture.

First, identify all possible structure markers. You have written out a verse on a sheet of paper. After you have identified and studied the longer, unusual, and repeated words and phrases (step 1), you may circle, underline, or highlight the little words, which give force to the big words. Use the following ordinary English sentence to practice these steps: "Ramesh came home from school to eat because he was hungry." The sentence has three little words as structure markers: *from, to,* and *because.*

Next, separate major structure markers from minor structure markers. Check the three structure markers above. All these words, *from, to,* and *because,* are not to be given equal weight in understanding the sentence, though they are all necessary to the meaning. *Because* is more important as a bone connector than *from* and *to. Because* connects two parts of the sentence. *From* connects only two words:

home and *school. To* connects *school* and *eat.* Separate the more important "bone connectors" from the less important ones.

Third, understand the meaning or the force of the major markers. For this step you will consult the chart "Grammatical Keys Indicating Structure" (pages 55–56). Sometimes you will have to separate the bones by attempting to understand them, and at other times you will only understand their force and function and use as you separate them.

In our sample sentence on Ramesh's consumption priorities, the word *because* carries the meaning of reason. The lesser important *from* refers to place in this context. *To* shows purpose.

Finally, outline the text according to the relative importance of the markers. Structuring a text will help you outline the text according to the emphasis of the author. The need to separate major structure keys from minor structure keys helps you understand the framework or skeleton that holds the details together.

When you structure the text according to the emphasis of the writer, you will seek to capture that emphasis in an outline. What you discern as big bones will fall toward the left side of the outline. The smaller bones will fall toward the right side of the outline. Your outline sequence should look like this:

    I.
      A.
         1.
            a.
               (1)
                  (a)
    II.
      A.
         1. (etc.)

The structural markers or bone connectors show the relative importance of the words they connect. Those of lesser importance will, in the outline, move toward the right side of the page.

    Major markers: Roman numerals—I, II, III
      Next level: Capital letters—A, B, C

> Next level: Arabic numerals—1, 2, 3
> Next level: Lowercase letters—a, b, c
> Next level: Numbers in parentheses—(1), (2), (3)
> Next level: Letters in parentheses—(a), (b), (c)

Our sample sentence, "Ramesh came home from school to eat because he was hungry," is divided into two parts, for there is one big bone connector: *because.*

> I. Ramesh came home
> II. The reason *(because):* he was hungry

There are two small bones, *from* and *to,* relating to the first part of the sentence. Thus you have two points at the next level of the outline in the first part of the sentence.

> I. Ramesh came home
>   A. Ramesh came home from school
>   B. Ramesh came home to eat
> II. The reason Ramesh came home was because he was hungry

Since there are no perceivable structural markers in the second part of the sentence, there are no second or third levels of the outline under II. In outlining you cannot have a third level without a second level, a fourth level without a third level, and so on. In outlining a text, you build on the previous level.

Let me illustrate structuring from the Ezra 7:10 text.

> For Ezra had set his heart to study the law of the LORD, and to practice it, and to teach His statues and ordinances in Israel.

First, identify all structure markers (little words that influence meaning). Here they are: *for, to, of, and, to, and, to, and.* Next, separate major from minor markers. Major markers in this verse are: *for, to, and, to, and, to.* The minor markers are any other markers that have been identified, for example, the third *and.*

Understand the meaning or the force of the more major markers.

- *For* relates this verse to the previous verse and does not have much to say about the structure of this particular verse.
- The word *to* is used three times and shows how the verse is to be divided into three.
- Major marker *and* is used twice—once between the first and second *to*, and between the second and third *to*. This also shows how the verse is put together.

Outline the text. Three main points can be derived from the grammar or content changes.

Ezra set his heart:

    I. to study the law of the Lord
      and
   II. to practice it
     and
  III. to teach
         a. his statutes
           and
         b. ordinances in Israel

Notice how the Ezra passage nicely divided into three points. The third point had two subpoints because of the minor structure marker *and* (the third *and*). The body of your sermon on this passage is already emerging.

Summarize the Main Sections of the Text

Summarizing is a very helpful exercise. It is basically a synopsis of the text that helps you understand the small section you are studying in the context of the Bible, chapter, section, or book. For instance, there are many details that a Bible writer may give to support a point. As you discern the movement of the text, you will note the major force of the text. Summarize each major force (they will be roman numerals in your outline) of the text so that you will eventually understand the main theme and thrust of the author.

Summarizing the passage will help you determine the dominant force of a text. It will also help you with the next step of the sermon-making process, that of structuring the text around the single theme/thrust or central proposition (step 3).

To summarize the text, go back to the outline you drafted when you analyzed the structure of the text. Summarize the thought contained at the major levels of the outline by putting it into a complete sentence.

The major sections of Ezra 7:10 can be summarized in the following way:

   I. Ezra set his heart to study the law of the Lord (v. 10a)
  II. Ezra set his heart to practice the law (v. 10b)
 III. Ezra set his heart to teach the law in Israel (v. 10c)
    A. He would teach the Lord's statutes
    B. He would teach the Lord's ordinances

Action Step

Let's go back to Ephesians 6:10–12 and apply step 2—structuring and summarizing—to it. You have already done step 1—studying the text, its words and relationships. As you study this section carefully, it will help you become an expository preacher who bases your authority on the Scriptures rather than on your own thoughts.

[10]*Finally,* be strong *in* the Lord, *and in* the strength *of* His might.

[11]Put on the whole armor *of* God, *that* you may be able *to* stand firm *against* the schemes *of* the devil.

[12]*For* our struggle is not *against* flesh *and* blood, *but against* the rulers, *against* the powers, *against* the world forces of this darkness, *against* the spiritual forces of wickedness in the heavenly places.

Structuring

You will do all four steps of structuring a passage: identify (italicized words in the text above), separate, understand, and outline. Please read these notes carefully with your Bible open to Ephesians 6:10–12.

Some Clues to the Verses

v. 10 *Finally* relates these verses to the previous text. It indicates that the author is starting a new thought and so is an important marker. *In* occurs twice and is of equal importance each time because the two occurrences of *in* are connected by the common joining word *and.* The two phrases *in the Lord* and *in the strength* will be given equal force in the outline. We have to decide what is the force or the meaning of the little word *in.* Go to the chart on grammatical keys on pages 55–56 to find that *in* denotes "means,"—that is, the means of being strong is in the Lord. *Of* is a very minor marker because it influences a phrase (his might) rather than the sentence.

With these clues, now attempt to structure verse 10.

v. 11 The first *of* is too minor to influence the whole sentence—it is part of the phrase "the armor of God." *That* is an important term. Our grammatical chart tells us that *that* may refer to reason, result, or purpose. Sometimes reason, result, and purpose may overlap. We can choose reason here, because in verse 12 the author gives a clear reason for putting on the armor of God. *To* is less important because it connects *able* to *stand firm. Against* is a word that is repeated several times in verses 11 and 12. It is not found in the grammatical keys chart because the chart is not comprehensive. Create the meaning of this word in your outline. You'll find many such words to which you must ascribe meaning. Again, the word *of* is quite minor. It is part of the phrase "schemes of the devil."

With these clues, now attempt to structure verse 11.

v. 12 The first word, *for,* is crucial. Notice that the translators decided to divide the thought by beginning a new verse here. This division often indicates an addition or change in structure. Now you have to decide if the break between verses 11 and 12 is as major as the break between verses 11 and 10. If it is a major break, then we have three points:

I.	v. 10
II.	v. 11
III.	v. 12

If the break is of less weight, then we have two points:

I.	v. 10
II.	vv. 11–12

For is clearly the reason for verse 11 and is part of the unit of thought begun in verse 11. *But* separates "flesh and blood" from the rest of our opposition. I am choosing the phrase "system of Satan" to denote all the rest of those terms. *Against* is repeated several times and clearly refers to the kinds of opposition that we may experience. Since *against* is repeated and is found in connection with the word *but,* it will influence our understanding of the different kinds of powers. Each of these kinds of opposition will be given equal weight in the outline.

With these clues, now attempt to structure verse 12.

Structure of the Verses

Here is my structure of Ephesians 6:10–12. Compare it to yours. Think through why mine looks the way it does. Why does yours look the way it does?
Major markers provide the major points.

I. *Finally* (v. 10)
II. The command to *put on* (vv. 11–12)

The next level of markers provides the subpoints.

I. *Finally* (v. 10)
    A. The means: *in* the Lord (v. 10a) and
    B. The means: *in* the strength of his might (v. 10b)
II. The command to *put on* (vv. 11–12)
    A. The first reason: *that* (v. 11)
    B. The second reason: *for* (v. 12)

Summarizing

Now summarize the main sections of this text. Attempt a summary of your main points on your own right now. And then think through why I summarized the main points the way I did.
Here is my summary:

I. The means of being strong is in the Lord and in his mighty strength (v. 10)
II. The reasons for putting on God's whole armor are to stand against Satan's schemes and struggle against Satan's system (vv. 11–12)

Notice that the summarization follows the force of the major structure markers.

My full structure and outline of Ephesians 6:10–12 follows. If you have understood the process to this point, you will understand the logic of my structure.

    I. The means of being strong is in the Lord and in his mighty strength (v. 10)

    A. We must be strong in the Lord (v. 10a)

    B. We must be strong in his mighty strength (v. 10b)

II. The reasons for putting on God's whole armor are to stand against Satan's schemes and to struggle against Satan's system (vv. 11–12)

    A. The first reason for putting on the whole armor of God is to stand firm against Satan's schemes (v. 11)

    B. The second reason for putting on the whole armor of God is to struggle against Satan's schemes (v. 11)

       1. Our struggle is not against flesh and blood (v. 12a)

       2. Our struggle is against Satan's system (v. 12b)

         a. Satan's system is comprised of rulers

         b. Satan's system is comprised of powers

         c. Satan's system is comprised of world forces

         d. Satan's system is comprised of spiritual forces in heavenly places

You now have a rather full outline of the text you desire to preach. This is a very helpful, authoritative means by which you can preach the Bible. Even if you do not go any further in the sermon-preparation process than step 2 and simply preach from the outline, you can be confident of being faithful to the Scriptures. However, if you do only this amount of work before going to the pulpit, your preaching will resemble a lecture rather than a sermon. Some very impactive aspects of expository preaching are yet to come. You must do the groundwork (steps 1 and 2) before climbing to step 3.

3

The Central
Proposition
of the Text

The "Heart" of the Text

Step 7: Preach the Sermon
Step 6: Structure the Sermon
Step 5: The Central Proposition of the Sermon
Step 4: The Purpose Bridge
Step 3: The Central Proposition of the Text
Step 2: Structure the Text
Step 1: Study the Text

Translators have divided biblical texts into paragraphs, each of which has one major, dominant, identifiable thought. In fact, the very definition of a paragraph is that it proposes one cardinal thought. This major thought is what I call the "central proposition of the text"

(CPT). Each central proposition is made up of two components: the theme and the thrust.

Our working definition of expository preaching sees its distinctiveness in "the contemporization of the central proposition of a biblical text." *The central proposition* is the heart of the text, which the preacher must discover. The central proposition is sometimes called by other names: "textual thrust," "exclusive emphasis," "sermonic screw," or the "big idea."[1]

Components of the Central Proposition

Theme (subject or topic)
Thrust (complement or assertions)

The central proposition is the singular theme/thrust around which the details of a biblical text are woven. Since we want to communicate one major point for the people to hear, understand, and obey, we seek to communicate the major proposition of each Scripture text in contemporary terms. If we leave our text (or sermon) to a chance perception of what this central proposition is, we are not really necessary in the dispensing and receiving of God's truth.

Listen to these masters on the subject of the central proposition.

> Reduce your text to a simple proposition, and lay that down as the warp; and then make use of the text itself as the woof; illustrating the main idea by the various terms in which it is contained. Screw the word into the minds of your hearers. A screw is the strongest of all mechanical powers . . . when it has turned a few times, scarcely any power can pull it out.
>
> Charles Simeon[2]

> A major affirmation of our definition of expository preaching, therefore, maintains that "expository preaching is the communication of a biblical concept." That affirms the obvious. . . . Ideally each sermon is the explanation, interpretation, or application of a single dominant idea supported by other ideas, all drawn from one passage or several passages of Scripture.
>
> Haddon Robinson[3]

Identifying the Central Proposition of the Text

The central proposition of the text is the single unit of thought that binds together and gives meaning to all the particulars of a text. Note that in step 5, "The Central Proposition of the Sermon," the same definition is given, except the last word is *sermon* rather than *text*.

What Does the CPT Look Like?

It is *always* in the form of a full grammatical sentence. If it is less than a sentence, it is not a proposition, by definition.

What Does the CPT Contain?

It has two components:

- The *theme* of the text: The theme of the text answers the question, What is the author talking about in the text?
- The *thrust* of the text: The thrust of the text answers the question, What is the author saying about what he is talking about in the text?

> Theme: What is the author talking about in the text?
> Thrust: What is the author saying about what he is talking about in the text?

From Where Does One Get the CPT?

The CPT is derived from step 2 when you structured the text. At each grammatical or content cue you made a division for a section. Minor grammatical or content cues determined subsections. Major content or grammatical cues determined the major sections. Each major section has a subject or single theme. The way the author relates these single themes will help you discover the central proposition of the larger text.

Let me illustrate, using Ephesians 4:7–16, and then you can apply it to the shorter passage of Ephesians 6:10–12. Read Ephesians 4:7–16 below three times before you go through this exercise. Read slowly and intentionally.

[7]But to each one of us grace was given according to the measure of Christ's gift.
[8]Therefore it says,
    "WHEN HE ASCENDED ON HIGH,
    HE LED CAPTIVE A HOST OF CAPTIVES,
    AND HE GAVE GIFTS TO MEN."
[9](Now this expression, "He ascended," what does it mean except that He also had descended into the lower parts of the earth?
[10]He who descended is Himself also He who ascended far above all the heavens, that He might fill all things.)
[11]And He gave some as apostles, and some as prophets, and some as evangelists, and some as pastors and teachers,
[12]for the equipping of the saints for the work of service, to the building up of the body of Christ;
[13]until we all attain to the unity of the faith, and of the knowledge of the Son of God, to a mature man, to the measure of the stature which belongs to the fullness of Christ.
[14]As a result, we are no longer to be children, tossed here and there by waves, and carried about by every wind of doctrine, by the trickery of men, by craftiness in deceitful scheming;
[15]but speaking the truth in love, we are to grow up in all aspects into Him, who is the head, even Christ,
[16]from whom the whole body, being fitted and held together by that which every joint supplies, according to the proper working of each individual part, causes the growth of the body for the building up of itself in love.

1. Verses 7–11 speak of one thing—the ascended Messiah gave gifts. (Remember that change in content is one of the cues for structuring a text.) Verses 7–11 address the same subject or single theme.
    Actually, you have to decide whether to break the text at verse 11 or verse 12. I have decided to break it at verse 12 since I am preaching the large text (vv. 7–16). If I were preaching from the

text twice, I would preach verses 7–10 and verses 11–16, emphasizing the grammatical key in the opening of verse 11.

2. Verses 12–13 tell us the purpose or reason he gave the gifts. Notice the key word *for* at the beginning of verse 12. Your grammatical keys chart (see pages 55–56) tells you that *for* communicates either reason or purpose. Here verses 12–13 give us the reason or purpose for Messiah giving the gifts. Again, these verses refer to the same subject or a singular theme. The gifts are given for the building up of the church till it reaches maturity.

3. Verses 14–16 tell us the result of this gift-giving process (vv. 7–13), explaining the implications of corporate maturity for which Messiah gave gifts. Notice the first phrase of verse 14, "as a result." The phrase controls verses 14–16 and shows the result of verses 7–13. These verses also carry the same subject or singular theme.

In order to get the central proposition of the text, you put the content of these three subjects, themes, main points, or summaries together. In arriving at the CPT, you are looking for *accuracy* and *adequacy*. The CPT must uniquely reflect your particular text and must cover the assertions of the text. It is essential to complete steps 1 and 2 on a text before tackling step 3.

Here is my CPT for Ephesians 4:7–16: The purpose for which the ascended Christ gave gifts to the church is to build it up to doctrinal maturity and functional stability by the working together of equipped believers.

Let's dissect this statement. Does it contain the theme (what the author is talking about) and the thrust (what the author is saying about what he is talking about)?

The Theme

The theme of a paragraph should be specific. If I asked you for the theme of the paragraph (What is the author talking about in Ephesians 4:7–16?) and you replied, "Spiritual gifts," you would be right but not *accurate*. Your theme could fit Romans 12; 1 Corinthians 12; or 1 Peter 4:7. You could say that the theme is "building up the body."

This time your theme would be right but not *adequate* to capture the whole paragraph.

To have a central theme that is both accurate and adequate, you must encompass in it the single themes or subjects from all your main points or summary statements. Grammatical or content cues will tell you which is the controlling theme—what the author is talking about. In this case the author is talking about the *purpose* for the giving of spiritual gifts by the ascended Messiah. If you did not include the words or concept of "the purpose" in the CPT, you are not being true to or precise with this passage.

The Thrust

What is the thrust of the theme? What is the author saying about the theme? He is saying that the purpose of gift giving is the building up of the church to doctrinal maturity and functional stability through the working together of equipped believers. Therefore, the full statement of the central proposition of this text is: The purpose for which the ascended Christ gave gifts to the church is to build it up to doctrinal maturity and functional stability by the working together of equipped believers.

Action Step

Now do the above exercise with Ephesians 6:10–12. Come up with the central proposition of that short paragraph—its theme and thrust.

Organizing Your Textual Work

At this point in the Scripture Sculpture process, you need to gather the details of your textual work (steps 1–3) into one or two pages. From here you will begin a sermonic ascent (steps 4–7). It will be well worth your time to organize your textual work in the following format (see sample forms below):

• Give a tentative title to the text. This could well be the "theme" of the CPT.

- If possible, write a personal translation or paraphrase of the text reflecting the flow or argument of the text. When you paraphrase the text, you must be sure to understand the way the author makes the argument. An example follows from Ephesians 4:11–13.
- Write out the central proposition of the text. (Put the theme and thrust in full-sentence form. The full statement does not need to be long, but make it adequate. You will refine it and shorten it as you work with it.)
- Write out the outline. (All points and subpoints should be in full sentences.)

Here you would be culminating the sermon-preparation process as far as the text itself is concerned.

Sample Form in Organizing Your Textual Work

Title of Passage

(Scripture Text)

Paraphrase or Translation

v. 1:

v. 2:

v. 3:

Central Proposition of the Text

Theme:

Thrust:

Full Statement. The full statement of the CPT puts the theme and thrust in one sentence.

Outline

    I.

        A.

            1.

            2.

        B.

            1.

            2.

    II.

        A.

        B.

            1.

            2.

            3.

        C.

    III.

Sample Form Applied to Ephesians 4:11–13

The Purpose of Divine Gift Giving
Ephesians 4:11–13

Paraphrase
[11]And He (the ascended Christ) gave some as apostles, and some as prophets, and some as evangelists, and some as pastors and teachers,
[12]for the (purpose of) equipping (preparing) of the saints for the work of service, to (with the result of) the building up of the body of Christ;
[13]until we all attain to the unity of the faith, and of the knowledge of the Son of God, to a mature man, to the measure of the stature which belongs to the fullness of Christ.

Central Proposition of the Text
Theme: The purpose for which the ascended Christ gave men as gifts to the church
Thrust: so that the church will be built up till it reaches Christ-like maturity
Full statement of the CPT: The purpose for which the ascended Christ gave these men as gifts is to build up the church till it reaches Christ-like maturity.

Outline
    I. The ascended Christ gave four classes of men as gifts to the church (v. 11)
       A. He gave some as apostles
       B. He gave some as prophets
       C. He gave some as evangelists
       D. He gave some as pastors and teachers
    II. The purpose for which he gave these men was so that the church will be built up (v. 12)
       A. These men were given for the purpose of equipping the saints for the work of service (v. 12a)
       B. Equipping the saints will result in the body being built up (v. 12b)
    III. The men were to equip the saints until the church reached corporate Christ-likeness (v. 13)
       A. They are to equip the saints until we all attain to the unity of the faith based on the knowledge of the Son of God (v. 13a)
       B. They are to equip the saints until we all attain to a mature man (v. 13b)
       C. They are to equip the saints until we all attain to the full measure of Christ-likeness (v. 13c)

Action Step

We will now review steps 1–3, using Psalm 117. Psalm 117, the shortest and simplest of the Psalms, is a favorite text to work with in our seminary classes. Read the psalm a couple of times before you study these next pages.

¹Praise the Lᴏʀᴅ, all nations;
  Laud Him, all peoples!
²For His lovingkindness is great toward us,
  And the truth of the Lᴏʀᴅ is everlasting.
  Praise the Lᴏʀᴅ!

Step 1: Study the Text

When you study the psalm, you will observe words like *praise, all, nations, peoples, lovingkindness,* and *truth of the Lᴏʀᴅ.* Studying the words will give you the flesh for your message.

Step 2: Structure the Text

You will notice that the crucial word for discerning the structure of the psalm is *for,* the first word in verse 2 (a grammatical key). The skeleton of your text could be this outline:

  I. The psalmist calls all people to praise the Lᴏʀᴅ (v. 1)
  II. The lovingkindness and truth of the Lᴏʀᴅ are to be praised (v. 2)

Step 3: The Central Proposition of the Text

What is the theme of this psalm? Think it through and then finish this sentence: In Psalm 117, the author is talking about _____
_____.

If you said that the author is speaking about "praising the Lord," you are only partially right, for you have not given adequate emphasis to the important grammatical key *for.* The author is not merely speaking about "praising the Lord" (that will be true of most thanksgiving psalms), he is speaking about "the reason why all peoples should praise the Lord." You get that emphasis from the first word in verse 2, *for.* (Have you checked the grammatical keys chart?)

Now, what is the thrust of the text? What is the author saying about what he is talking about? Finish this sentence: The reason why all peoples should praise the Lord is _____
_____.

If you did the work, you would come up with something like the following for the full statement of the CPT of Psalm 117: The reason there should be universal praise of the Lord is because of his lovingkindness and eternal truth.

Think through the above statement. Can you see how I arrived at it? If you really desire to be an expositor of the Word of God, you will seek to impress on your people what the author stresses—the truth of his text. In order to find that specific central proposition, this proven, and perhaps tedious, exercise has to be used. Yet this is a wonderful way of making the text a part of your own being. You will not even have to memorize the text. You will know it very well by the time you are ready to preach it.

Action Step

Try a central proposition of the text for the following Bible passages.
Ephesians 6:1–4
[1]Children, obey your parents in the Lord, for this is right.
[2]Honor your father and mother (which is the first commandment with a promise),
[3]That it may be well with you, and that you may live long on the earth.
[4]And, fathers, do not provoke your children to anger; but bring them up in the discipline and instruction of the Lord.

Theme: _____

_____

Thrust: _____

_____

CPT: _____

_____

What would be the central proposition of the text for just verses 1–3?
Ephesians 6:1–3

Theme: _____

_____

Thrust: _____

_____

CPT: _____

_____

What about the central proposition of the text for just verse 4?
Ephesians 6:4

Theme: _____

_____

Thrust: _____

_____

CPT: _____

_____

You have already worked on the CPT for Ephesians 6:10–12. Write it here:
Ephesians 6:10–12

Theme: _____

_____

Thrust: _____

_____

CPT: _____

_____

4

THE PURPOSE BRIDGE

The "Brain" of the Sermon

Step 7: Preach the Sermon
Step 6: Structure the Sermon
Step 5: The Central Proposition of the Sermon
Step 4: The Purpose Bridge
Step 3: The Central Proposition of the Text
Step 2: Structure the Text
Step 1: Study the Text

We now come to the most critical part of the entire sermon-preparation process. When you cross this bridge, you will have gone from studying the Scriptures—a hermeneutical exercise—toward preaching the Scriptures—the homiletical exercise. Step 4 is when you construct and cross the *purpose bridge*.[1] Step 4 is critical to making expository preaching relevant to the audience. By this time, much of the spadework for the sermon has already been done. The flesh (step 1), the skeleton (step 2), and the heart (step 3) of the text have been discerned. The skeleton of the body of the sermon has been formed with the main points, subpoints, and sub-subpoints following the grammatical and content keys found in the passage.

Thus we come to the brain or the *purpose* of the sermon.[2]

The Purpose of Purpose

As the brain of the sermon, the purpose controls many aspects of sermon preparation and preaching. Here are a few. A valid and clear purpose of the sermon

- focuses the introduction of the sermon on the need that will be raised in the sermon
- determines what must be included and/or excluded in the body of the sermon
- influences the sermon's conclusion and any application
- helps in choosing the illustrations that will help accomplish the purpose of the sermon
- provides a more objective way to measure the proficiency or success of the sermon
- most importantly, directly contributes to the form of the theme of the central proposition of the sermon (CPS)

I cannot exaggerate the importance of the purpose of the sermon as the key link from text to sermon.[3]

Determining the Purpose of the Sermon

How does one go about finding and articulating the purpose of the sermon?[4] We find the purpose of the sermon (construct the purpose bridge) by asking and answering the following question: *On the basis of the central proposition of this text, what does God want my people to understand and obey?*

Notice that the purpose of the *text* is not the primary consideration here. That purpose already would have influenced the study process in determining the central proposition of the text as you considered the details and context of the passage. Of course, the purpose of the sermon will be compatible with the expectations of the biblical author(s) of their original audiences. We are preserved from whim and error in the purpose bridge since we have followed the study process in steps 1 through 3.

Connecting the Purpose of Your Sermon and the Purpose of Your Text

When you write out the purpose for your sermon built on the central proposition of the text, you need to answer two *compatibility questions.*

1. Can I make an exegetical or theological case that my sermon's purpose is compatible with the *purpose* of the text? This question enables one to be faithful to the text.
2. Can I make a sociological or psychological case that my sermon's purpose is compatible with the *needs* of my audience? This question enables one to be relevant to the audience.

The central proposition of the text is solidly based on the passage to be preached. Now, based on the central proposition of the text, what can I hope to accomplish in the sermon concerning the people's understanding and obedience?

It is essential to be well acquainted with your audience. As you construct the purpose bridge, ask this critical question: What are the needs and condition of my audience in reference to the central proposition of this text?[5]

You can know your audience only by spending time with them. There are no good sermons that are generic to every audience. "Long-distance" shepherding is neither biblically approved nor congregationally appreciated.

The Purpose Bridge
Number 1 Issue: What are the needs and condition of my audience?

I will illustrate step 4 from two biblical texts, Isaiah 19:18–25 and Ephesians 4:7–16. Then you can apply it to Ephesians 6:10–12.

Isaiah 19:18–25

[18]In that day five cities in the land of Egypt will be speaking the language of Canaan and swearing allegiance to the LORD of hosts; one will be called the City of Destruction.

[19]In that day there will be an altar to the LORD in the midst of the land of Egypt, and a pillar to the LORD near its border.

[20]And it will become a sign and a witness to the LORD of hosts in the land of Egypt; for they will cry to the LORD because of oppressors, and He will send them a Savior and a Champion, and He will deliver them.

[21]Thus the LORD will make Himself known to Egypt, and the Egyptians will know the LORD in that day. They will even worship with sacrifice and offering, and will make a vow to the LORD and perform it.

[22]And the LORD will strike Egypt, striking but healing; so they will return to the LORD, and He will respond to them and will heal them.

[23]In that day there will be a highway from Egypt to Assyria, and the Assyrians will come into Egypt and the Egyptians into Assyria, and the Egyptians will worship with the Assyrians.

[24]In that day Israel will be the third party with Egypt and Assyria, a blessing in the midst of the earth,

[25]whom the LORD of hosts has blessed, saying, "Blessed is Egypt My people, and Assyria the work of My hands, and Israel My inheritance."

A Middle Eastern crisis captivated the entire world in early 1991. Mixed feelings of helplessness and conquest, pity and power, pain and disdain were highly evident throughout the United States. I had to preach at the chapel services of Dallas Seminary and Wheaton College at this very critical time. Both schools had constituents who were for and against the war in the Gulf.

The text I chose was Isaiah 19:18–25. After pursuing steps 1 and 2, I arrived at step 3.

The central proposition of this text is as follows: The Middle Eastern enemies of Israel will be converted to covenant status with YHWH in the future kingdom.

The central proposition of this prophetic text, as it stands, is distant (past and future!) but still is in the Scripture. It must be preached, because all Scripture is inspired and beneficial.

The purpose bridge (step 4) will help me discern the focus and force of my eventual sermon. Many purposes can be preached from this text. After asking the compatibility questions, I wrote down a few:

1. To prove that God's salvation grace will one day reach to the enemies of Israel
2. To provide hope that the Middle East political problem will one day be solved

These purposes were compatible and appropriate to the Scripture and my audience. If I accomplished these purposes, I still would have taught the Bible and offered some hope for the audience.

I would love to preach purpose 1 to an audience of Jewish believers from their Old Testament. I have taught purpose 2 to an audience of Arab believers in the Middle East. But I decided to pursue a third purpose. This purpose too must be compatible with the text (the Bible) and the audience (a hurting and divided U.S. audience). I came up with the following: 3. To enable my audience to transcend present historical war trauma by embracing God's plans for the Middle East in the future kingdom.

Note that you can have more than one purpose, and therefore more than one sermon per text, but not an unlimited number of them. You are both liberated and limited by the central proposition of the text. You can have as many nuanced sermons as the number of purposes the central proposition of the text permits. You must choose the sermonic purpose and fine tune it to the audience to whom you minister.[6]

Ephesians 4:7–16

There are at least three purposes one can preach from the central proposition of Ephesians 4:7–16 (check your notes from step 3 for that CPT). Here are the purposes:

1. To inform people of the giftedness of every believer in the body of Christ
2. To challenge church leaders to equip the believers to serve
3. To challenge believers to understand and apply God's every-member plan for the building of the body in their churches

I chose purpose number 3 based on a general factor and a specific factor. In general I would rather preach a behavioral purpose than a mere cognitive purpose. Usually the behavioral purpose is built on biblical information so that I can accomplish faithfulness to the cognitive or content purpose as well as asking for change in the hearer's life.

Specifically I needed to take my church audience and church needs into account. Purpose 3 fit well into my church situation. In other places when I address only church leaders, I pursue purpose 2. That is, I can preach the same text in two ways to two different audiences, though substantial parts of the sermon would be similar.

Action Step

Before you read on, come up with a purpose bridge based on your central proposition of Ephesians 6:10–12. Take your audience needs and condition into account. Construct a purpose bridge beginning with the word "to. . . ." Purpose statements will always contain the word *to*. You may have several possible purposes for your CPT. Now read on.

The central proposition of this text (step 3) would look something like this:

Theme: The reasons for putting on the whole armor of God's mighty strength
Thrust: . . . enables us to stand against the schemes of the devil and to struggle against the system of the devil
Full statement: Putting on the whole armor of the Lord's mighty strength enables us to stand against the schemes of the devil and to struggle against the system of the devil.

What are some purposes that you can preach from this central proposition (step 4)? Here are a couple:

1. To inform people about the devil's works and ways
2. To motivate people to put on the armor of the Lord's strength in their struggle against the devil

Both of these purposes are legitimately drawn from this text. The first is content oriented; the second is behavior oriented. I would choose the second purpose for two reasons. One, while accomplishing the behavioral purpose, I could cover the content purpose. Also, the purpose of this text is wider than just dissemination of content. Two, my audience's needs are more in line with how to fight Satan than with just finding out about him. More precisely, the purpose is not to show them the *what* and *how* of putting on the whole armor of God—that comes in verses 13–17. We strictly stay with the purposes that the central proposition of the text affords—why they should put on God's armor of strength.

A hint for the next step (step 5): Your purpose statement will almost always, in raw form, provide the *theme* of the central proposition of the sermon.

5

THE CENTRAL
PROPOSITION
OF THE SERMON

The "Heart" of the Sermon

Step 7: Preach the Sermon
Step 6: Structure the Sermon
Step 5: The Central Proposition of the Sermon
Step 4: The Purpose Bridge
Step 3: The Central Proposition of the Text
Step 2: Structure the Text
Step 1: Study the Text

In steps 1–3 we found the raw materials and the central proposition in the text. We have formulated the direction in which that proposition needs to be shaped in order to impact our people (step 4). The next three steps will yield the finished product that you will preach.

Steps 5–7 are fundamental steps as well. You could do steps 1–3 and teach biblical truth. You could add step 4 and proclaim biblical demands. But steps 5–7 enable you to proclaim biblical truth and application in a relevant and persuasive manner.

In step 5 we deal with the *central proposition of the sermon* (CPS). Here the central proposition of the text (step 3) is channeled through the purpose (step 4). It is then contemporized by the central proposition of the sermon to bring about obedience to God's claims. The CPS takes you into the homiletical aspects of the sermon-preparation process.

Enjoy some well-known preachers speaking to the importance of the central proposition of the sermon:

> For the sermon, as a living word from God to his people, should make its impact on them then and there. They will not remember the details. We should not expect them to do so. But they should remember the dominant thought, because all the sermon's details have been marshalled to help them grasp its message and feel its power.
>
> John R. W. Stott[1]

> The subject answers the question, What is the sermon about? . . . Whether a sermon has two points or ten points, it must have one point; it must be about something.
>
> John A. Broadus[2]

> The first thing in making a sermon, the sine qua non, is the idea. There can be no sermon that was not first preceded by an idea or a theme. The novelist Henry James called the idea in story writing the "germ." It is the bacterial beginning, the point of conception, he said, for every work of art or creation. The same is true for the idea of the sermon; it is the germ, the insight, from which eventually the entire sermon is grown.
>
> John Killinger[3]

J. H. Jowett's lines on this subject from his "Yale Lectures on Preaching" are famous (quoted by Stott, Robinson, and others):

> I have a conviction that no sermon is ready for preaching, not ready for writing out, until we can express its theme in a short, pregnant sen-

tence as clear as crystal. I find the getting of that sentence is the hardest, the most exacting, and the most fruitful labour in my study. To compel oneself to fashion that sentence, to dismiss every word that is vague, ragged, ambiguous, to think oneself through to a form of words which defines the theme with scrupulous exactness—this is surely one of the most vital and essential factors in the making of a sermon: and I do not think any sermon ought to be preached or even written, until that sentence has emerged, clear and lucid as a cloudless moon.

J. H. Jowett[4]

Coming Up with the CPS

It is easy to emphasize the necessity and importance of the central proposition of the sermon. The problem of course is to come up with it! The series of steps in the Scripture Sculpture process should give you a mechanism by which you may arrive at the central proposition of the sermon. These steps build on each other, and they are sequential.

The process is thoroughly integrated. Our study (step 1) and structure (step 2) influence the central proposition of the text (step 3). The CPT influences the purpose of the sermon (step 4). From the purpose of the sermon, we have to articulate the central proposition of the sermon (step 5).

You already know the mechanics of finding the central proposition (see step 3). Just as the text has a singular theme/thrust, your sermon must have a singular theme/thrust as well.[5] For the CPS, you ask the key questions of yourself rather than of the biblical author.

The Central Proposition of the Sermon

Theme: What am I talking about?
Thrust: What am I saying about what I am talking about?

Here is a major hint for developing your theme: *It is often possible to turn the purpose of the sermon into the theme of the sermon.*

I will illustrate, using the CPT of Ephesians 4:11–16. (Note that I am doing this step only for verses 11–16 to illustrate that we could study segments of a paragraph as worthy of an entire sermon. Further, I don't want to give you all the answers right away! Could you distinguish between the CPT of verses 7–16 and verses 11–16?)

Step 3   *Theme:* Christ's plan for building the church to maturity
         Thrust: Will equip all believers to grow and function in the body
Step 4   The purpose of the sermon (the purpose may take any number of twists within the parameters of the CPT): To challenge believers to apply Christ's every-member plan for the spiritual building of their congregation
Step 5   The central proposition of the sermon (in raw form, we can turn the purpose into the theme of the CPS in the form of a question): What is Christ's every-member plan for the building up of the body?
         It is here we begin to "contemporize" the raw central proposition of the sermon into an even catchier homiletical style. But the germinal truth we will be preaching about is "Christ's every-member plan for the building up of Christ's body."

Note that the thrust of the CPS may take a number of forms:

1. The theme may have to be *proved,* addressing the question: Does this divine plan really result in the building of the body? Proof would certainly be the main emphasis if one was preaching only verses 11 through 16.
2. The theme may have to be *explained,* as in the case of the theme and thrust given above. The points in the sermon will explain this theme or even the whole proposition.
3. The CPS may have a *multiple thrust* to the theme. For example, in Ephesians 4:7–16 the theme "Christ's Plan for the Maturity of the Church" has three dimensions:

          Thrust: 1 . . . (vv. 7–11)
                     2 . . . (vv. 12–13)
                     3 . . . (vv. 14–16)

I chose the latter "multiple thrust" as the form of my CPS since the passage easily divided into three. We discerned this easy division from the structure of the passage (see step 2, page 69).

I put forward the following as the central proposition of the sermon from Ephesians 4:7–16:

Theme: The divine blueprint for body building
Thrust: 1. The Lord's responsibility is to endow the church (4:7–11).
         2. The leader's responsibility is to equip the church (4:12–13).
         3. The laity's responsibility is to enable the church (4:14–16).

You may want to compare this central proposition with step 3 on the same text given earlier (page 69).

Contemporization

Several angles must be probed in contemporization.[6]

Contemporization of the Proposition

You will note that in the CPS I developed above—The Divine Blueprint for Body Building—I tried to "contemporize" the statement with some catchy words, *blueprint* and *body building,* that would more vividly communicate my proposition. To contemporize is "to make contemporary." These "contemporizations" stick in the hearer's mind. The theme of the CPS doubled as my sermon title.

Contemporization of Words

This is basically an updating of vocabulary for effect and impact. Perhaps we would use a few easily memorable or metaphor-laden words. There is no limit to how much the preacher can use his imagination and audience in finding impacting words for a sermonic central proposition.

Contemporization of Audience

You are not speaking to the Ephesians or to Moses' audience. You are speaking to your own congregation. Your CPS and main points have to be personalized. For instance, instead of saying, "The Ephesians were challenged . . . ," you would say, "We are challenged." Your sermon's central proposition allows your sermon to be a laser beam directed to this specific audience rather than a floodlight directed to a generic audience. The CPS is always based on the text as the authoritative light source.

Check appendix 5, "The Perils of Principilization," to be sure that you are not simply universalizing the central proposition to the widest possible abstraction for the sake of relevance. Again, you could lose the uniqueness and specificity of the text if you are attempting to always universalize a proposition, to principlize it into some timeless truth. I heard a sermon on Abraham from Hebrews 11, which spoke about how to be a good father. I am not against being a good father. I also do not question the relevance of the subject to the audience. The issue is, Does the text warrant the theme? It did not. Consequently, it was a fine sermon on a "hot" topic but without authority from the text that was supposedly the basis for it.

You will also contemporize your application from this central proposition. This will be covered in step 6, "Structuring the Sermon."

Alliteration

In the threefold thrust of my central proposition of Ephesians 4:7–16, I have tried to alliterate important words so that people can remember the main points: *Lord's, leader's, laity's; endow, equip, enable.* While contemporization is always good and necessary, alliteration may not be so. Sometimes preachers think that they must alliterate everything. Alliteration is to help the sermon, not to harass the text! Alliteration is good if it makes the central proposition and main points less obscure and more memorable.

An Illustration of Contemporization

Keep pursuing the contemporization of words for your audience so that the CPS can be remembered and is pertinent to your people. This is a "style" issue. As you gain an understanding of your audience, you will know how to express your central proposition in their terms and categories of understanding. I here illustrate the process using Revelation 4:1–11. Read the passage to understand my CPT.

[1]After these things I looked, and behold, a door standing open in heaven, and the first voice which I had heard, like the sound of a trumpet speaking with me, said, "Come up here, and I will show you what must take place after these things."

[2]Immediately I was in the Spirit; and behold, a throne was standing in heaven, and One sitting on the throne.

[3]And He who was sitting was like a jasper stone and a sardius in appearance; and there was a rainbow around the throne, like an emerald in appearance.

[4]And around the throne were twenty-four thrones; and upon the thrones I saw twenty-four elders sitting, clothed in white garments, and golden crowns on their heads.

[5]And from the throne proceed flashes of lightning and sounds and peals of thunder. And there were seven lamps of fire burning before the throne, which are the seven Spirits of God;

[6]and before the throne there was, as it were, a sea of glass like crystal; and in the center and around the throne, four living creatures full of eyes in front and behind.

[7]And the first creature was like a lion, and the second creature like a calf, and the third creature had a face like that of a man, and the fourth creature was like a flying eagle.

[8]And the four living creatures, each one of them having six wings, are full of eyes around and within; and day and night they do not cease to say,

"HOLY, HOLY, HOLY, is THE LORD GOD, THE ALMIGHTY,
who was and who is and who is to come."

[9]And when the living creatures give glory and honor and thanks to Him who sits on the throne, to Him who lives forever and ever,

[10]the twenty-four elders will fall down before Him who sits on the throne, and will worship Him who lives forever and ever, and will cast their crowns before the throne, saying,

> [11]"Worthy art Thou, our Lord and our God, to receive glory and honor and power; for Thou didst create all things, and because of Thy will they existed, and were created."

Step 3—the CPT: The exclusive throne right of God to rule over the affairs of history is recognized by the residents of heaven.

Step 4—the purpose: I could go several ways with this proposition, especially as I take into consideration the early audience to whom John wrote. Do you remember the compatibility questions of step 4 (see p. 79)? Here are two possible purposes that will shape different sermons:

1. To encourage believers who are presently being persecuted (just as the passage would have encouraged those who were persecuted during John's time or will encourage those in the future tribulation) with the omnipotent rule of God over history.
2. To challenge believers to relinquish throne rights to their lives. Again, we must ask the compatibility questions. I can make a case that John's revelation was to confront those who think they rule the affairs of life such as Caesar then or Antichrist in the future.

I chose the second purpose. My audience was strongly tempted to play the role of God in their own lives.

Step 5—the CPS: I came up with an initial CPS. Notice how the purpose was turned into the theme of the central proposition of the sermon in the form of a question.

Theme: Why should you not attempt to occupy heaven's throne; or, why should you not play the role of God?
Thrust: Because the creatures of heaven recognize that God alone occupies that sovereign throne position.

This theme and thrust would accurately reflect the text and be adequately relevant to my audience, but I wanted to phrase the CPS in a catchier, more memorable way. (This did not keep me from sprinkling the more formal CPS through my talk.)

After some deliberation, I contemporized my theme to: "Get Off the Chair!" Because I use this phrase throughout the sermon—in the introduction, body, and conclusion—the audience will remember it. The phrase also has applicational power. In fact, I apply it to myself, reminding myself to "get off the chair" when I occasionally flirt with temptations to self-deification!

Action Step

Work with Ephesians 6:10–12 as an artist would—think, reflect, meditate, make, and remake a fitting sermon proposition. I suggest you do it before continuing in this manual. Here is my attempt at applying the process proposed in this method of sermon preparation.

Step 3—CPT:	The reasons for putting on the whole armor of the Lord's mighty strength are to stand against the schemes of the devil and to struggle against the system of the devil.
Step 4—Purpose:	To motivate people to put on the armor of the Lord's strength in their struggle against the devil.
Step 5—CPS:	Turn the purpose into the theme of the CPS.
Theme:	Why should Christians put on the whole armor of the Lord's strength?
Thrust:	To stand against the devil's schemes and to struggle against the devil's system.

At this point, it may well be worth it to contemporize the theme into a homiletically memorable phrase. You could reword the theme and thrust as follows:

Theme:	Why sovereign strength is sufficient for your strategy against Satan.
Thrust:	It enables you to stand against his schemes and struggle against his system.

6

STRUCTURE
THE SERMON

The "Skeleton" of the Sermon

Step 7: Preach the Sermon
Step 6: Structure the Sermon
Step 5: The Central Proposition of the Sermon
Step 4: The Purpose Bridge
Step 3: The Central Proposition of the Text
Step 2: Structure the Text
Step 1: Study the Text

All sermons, generally speaking, divide into three movements—introduction, body, and conclusion. "Structuring" the sermon relates to all three movements and to each movement. The process of developing these movements separately and together makes for structuring the sermon.

There are several ways to develop the three movements of a sermon, but any way in which one structures a sermon must exhibit unity, order, and progress. Unity is found by orienting the entire sermon process around the central proposition of the text, the purpose bridge, and the central proposition of the sermon.[1] Order and progress need to be demonstrated through the design structure and body structure of the sermon. The design structure of the sermon relates to meeting the purpose you established in step 4. The body structure of the sermon relates to the arrangement of the parts within the body of the sermon to reflect the text you are preaching.

Often the outline of the body of the sermon will follow the major divisions (but not the exact words or necessarily the sequence) of the text's outline in step 2. It will be necessary to contemporize the outline of the body of the sermon for the contemporary audience. Work hard to make the words of the text come alive to contemporary ears.

Basically, sermons are developed in one of two ways: deductively or inductively. A simple way of distinguishing between these two is by seeing where the central proposition of the sermon is placed. In a deductive sermon the CPS is fully stated *before* you actually get into the body of the sermon. In an inductive sermon the CPS is fully stated at the *end* as summary or proof of your sermon. There is a great deal of variety and versatility in arrangement as long as you are able to communicate the sermon's central proposition and explain it from the text.

Big Bones and Small Bones

You may recall the analogy of the big bones and small bones in step 2. In step 6 we must also do some "bone setting" to structure the sermon.

The big bones of your sermon are the introduction, the body, and the conclusion. The medium-sized bones of your sermon are the sub-introduction and the main points of the body. The smaller bones are the subpoints between the main points. The main points could have subpoints and sub-subpoints and more as you work out the design of the sermon. We will flesh out this skeleton when we write the sermon (step 7).

The Bones in Sermons

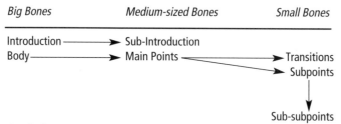

Conclusion

A sermon usually follows an arrangement similar to the one in the following chart. Attempt to understand the arrangement before proceeding to the rest of this chapter.

Sermon Structure

Title of Sermon
Bible Text
I. Introduction to the Sermon
   A. Sub-Introduction
II. Body of the Sermon
   A. First main section
      1. First subsection
         a. First sub-subsection
         b. Second sub-subsection
      2. Second subsection
   B. Second main section
      1. First subsection
      2. Second subsection
   C. Third main section
III. Conclusion

Remember that the three big bones are the critical movements of a sermon—the introduction, the body, and the conclusion. Within these movements there are secondary movements. The number of these secondary movements will vary. The big bones—the introduction, body, and conclusion—are the design structure. The parts of the body of the sermon—sections, subsections, and sub-

subsections—are the body structure, the part of the sermon that deals with the biblical text.

This distinction between body structure and design structure enables us to answer another question that is raised about biblical preaching. Should a sermon be text oriented or audience oriented? To an extent, the question is mute in reference to the sermon-preparation method proposed here. The CPT preserves the text from the preacher's whim. For the sake of the question, however, I would like to suggest that the form of the movements of the sermon (the design structure) is audience oriented (this along with the wording of the CPS and main points). The content of the body structure is text oriented. Audience orientation affects the formal and/or external aspects of the sermon. Text orientation affects the content and internal aspects of the sermon. In no case should the sermon be preacher oriented!

Text Orientation *As the sermon relates to the text*	Audience Orientation *As the sermon relates to the audience*
• Statement of CPT	• Purpose of sermon
	• Statement of CPS
	• Structure of the entire sermon
• Sub-introduction	• Introduction
• Structure of the sermon's body	• Application
	• Conclusion

Action Step

Now we can fill in some details of the sermon structure as was outlined in the chart on page 97. Please study this section carefully.

Title of Sermon
Bible Text

Main Introduction to the Sermon
The CPS is placed at the end of the introduction if it is a deductive sermon. In an inductive sermon, just your theme will be stated here.
Sub-Introduction
Many aspects could be covered here. Give background, provide context, make a

transition to the body; introduce the main sections; restate the CPS or theme; tell how the text is to be divided; state the central proposition of the text or make mention of the first main point or section of the sermon.

Body of the Sermon
   I. First main section (The number of main sections in the body of the sermon normally depends on the number of main points your text yielded when you structured it in step 2.) Be sure to introduce the subsections of this main section.
     A. First subsection
       Optional: Introduce the sub-subsections of this subsection if it will not be tedious and if you so desire.
       1. First sub-subsection
       2. Second sub-subsection
         Optional: Review the sub-subsections 1 and 2.
     B. Second subsection
       At this point, be sure to review the CPS (in a deductive sermon) or theme (in an inductive sermon) or the preceding subsections and/or the first in a section. Then transition to the second main section.
  II. Second main section (Do the same as you did with the first main section.) Be sure to introduce the subsections of this main section.
     A. First subsection
     B. Second subsection
       At this point, be sure to review the CPS (in a deductive sermon) or theme (in an inductive sermon) or the preceding subsections and/or the preceding main sections. Then transition to the next main section.
  III. Third main section (Do the same as you did in the first two sections.) The central proposition of the sermon is fully stated here in an inductive sermon. The CPS is repeated here for emphasis and review in a deductive sermon. You then move to the conclusion.
Conclusion

Action Step

The following is an example of the sermon structure from a text we used in step 5. My notes in parentheses are for your understanding of the process. Study this section carefully with your Bible open and while referring to steps 1–5 in this book.

Body Building
Ephesians 4:7–16

Introduction
   (Introduce the need for growth and functioning of our church body—or "Body building.")

Theme of the CPS: What is the divine blueprint for the growth and functioning of the body?

Sub-Introduction

Thrust of the CPS: (Introduce three aspects of the divine plan. Repeat the first aspect of the divine plan and then proceed to the first point in the body of the sermon.)

Body
  I. The Lord's responsibility is to endow the church (vv. 7–11)
     (Introduce the two kinds of endowment that the Lord undertakes.)
     A. Christ gave gifts to men (vv. 7–10)
     B. Christ gave gifts of men (v. 11)
        (Introduce the four classes of gifts of men that the Lord endows.)
        1. He gave apostles (v. 11a)
        2. He gave prophets (v. 11b)
        3. He gave evangelists (v. 11c)
        4. He gave pastor-teachers (v. 11d)
 II. The leaders' responsibility is to equip the church (vv. 12–13)
     (Introduce the leaders' responsibility in a church: *What* we are supposed to do and *how long* we are to do it.)
     A. What is the leaders' responsibility? Equip the church (v. 12)
        1. Equipping of the saints (v. 12a)
        2. For the work of service (v. 12b)
        3. To the building up of the body (v. 12c)
     B. How long are they to do it? Until the church looks like Jesus (v. 13)
        1. Corporate unity (v. 13a)
        2. Corporate maturity (v. 13b)
        3. Corporate Christ-likeness (v. 13c)
III. The laity's responsibility is to enable the church (vv. 14–16)
     (Introduce the two aspects of the people's responsibility.)
     A. They are no longer to be spiritual children (v. 14)
        1. Spiritual children are unstable
        2. Spiritual children are gullible
     B. They are to grow up to spiritual adulthood (vv. 15–16)
        1. Grow up in knowledge (v. 15)
        2. Grow up in service (v. 16)
Conclusion

Comments on the structure of the body of the sermon:

1. All main points are in full sentences. They are not just dangling words or hanging topics without the context of a sentence. As much as possible, put the subpoints in full sentences as well.

2. The main points have a degree of symmetry. This symmetry should arise from the text and is pursued in the presentation.
3. All sermons do not have three main points. We find that many sermons do. The number of main points depends on the number of main points in the text.

We go on to the passage we have been working on: Ephesians 6:10–12. Here is a possible sermon body structure of this passage.

I. God's extraordinary strength is accessible to the ordinary Christian (vv. 10–11a)
  A. You must be strong (v. 10)
    1. You must be strong in the Lord (v. 10a)
    2. You must be strong in the strength of his might (v. 10b)
  B. You must put on the whole armor of God (v. 11a)
II. God's extraordinary strength is sufficient for your strategy against Satan (vv. 11b–12)
  A. Putting on God's armor of strength enables you to stand against Satan's schemes (v. 11b)
  B. Putting on God's armor of strength enables you to struggle against Satan's system (v. 12)
    1. Satan's system is not flesh and blood
    2. Satan's system is a supernatural hierarchy
      a. There are rulers
      b. There are powers
      c. There are wicked forces
      d. There are spiritual forces

The Parts of a Sermon

Now that we have looked into the body structure of the sermon, I would like us to look at the design structure. We are now getting into deeper aspects of the homiletical undertaking.

Title

Your sermon needs a title, and your title will emerge in the sermon at various times. If you have worked hard on contemporizing your sermon's central proposition, you could use the theme (of that central proposition) itself as the title. In my example from Revelation 4, I use "Get Off the Chair!" as my title as well as my theme.

Your title must be an advertisement with attention-getting impact. Just as artists give titles to their works, the title is the identity you give to a sermon. It needs to be accurate—don't promise more than you can deliver. I once spoke on "How to See God," and the non-Christian community came to find out the answer. I may have promised too much in that title! Your title needs to be interesting. A question often evokes intrigue. The title also needs to be clear and short. Natural spots to highlight your title would be during the introduction, in the theme statement of the CPS, or in the concluding movement.

Reading the Bible Text

It is good to declare the actual text that you are preaching so that those who wish to follow along in the Bible will be able to do so. You have several options for when to declare and read the text.

- You may declare the text in your weekly bulletin. If you announce the text for the following week, people can read it before coming to church. Or you can cultivate the reading of the text among those who habitually come early to your services.
- Somebody can read the Scripture in the early part of the service before you get up to preach. On occasion, the text can be read responsively.
- You may make some preliminary remarks before you actually begin the sermon. Announcing the text (if it has been read before) or reading the text at this time provides a good transition to the sermon. Announce the text at least two times. Give the congregation a moment to find the text and announce it a third time during the move from your introduction to sub-introduction.
- You can announce the text at the end of your preliminary remarks (I call this the "pre-introduction"—see below) but actually read the pertinent verses only when you are expounding it.

Introduction

Your introduction has three dimensions to it: pre-introduction, main introduction, and sub-introduction.

Pre-Introduction

Ordinarily, pre-introductory comments are necessary. Perhaps someone has sung a song and needs a compliment (or at least an acknowledgment if it was not well done!). Or perhaps you need to affirm a public announcement. Or maybe you are a guest speaker and want to make preliminary remarks of gratitude for the opportunity to speak to your audience.

These kinds of remarks may be made in the pre-introduction section of your introduction. They do not have anything to do with your sermon but are indispensable in creating an environment of acceptance and in demonstrating that you have been paying attention to the larger issues of that service and the church. You need to convey warmth and friendship to the audience. You may ask them to open their Bibles and follow along as you read your passage. At the end of the pre-introduction, you may want to pray.

By bringing your pre-introduction to a close by pausing a moment or by praying, you will signal to the audience that you are about to start your sermon. Give them a cue that you are now moving into the introduction.

Main Introduction

I cannot emphasize enough the role that a strong main introduction has to play in the effectiveness of the sermon. If you do not have your audience yearning (within the first few minutes) for the rest of the sermon, they might as well go home. A strong main introduction has four ingredients. They are an integrated package and are not given here in any special order. An effective main introduction must accomplish these four goals.

Get attention. In one sense, getting the attention of the audience is the easiest of the four ingredients to accomplish. Attention is already being paid to the speaker as he walks up to the pulpit to preach. To maintain audience attention, however, the speaker must raise a relevant need.

Raise need. The most important part of the main introduction is helping the audience sense a need to hear the issues you will address in the sermon. Raising the need is a critical contemporization strategy. Spend a good amount of preparation and preaching time articulating the need the sermon meets. One way to measure a good sermon is to think through how relevant the need is and how well the sermon met that need.

What need should one raise? And where does the preacher get the ideas for his need? In the scheme that has been set forth, he gets the need from the purpose that has been stated in step 4. This is another reason why the importance of the purpose bridge cannot be exaggerated. The purpose not only provides the theme of the central proposition of the sermon but also provides the need to be raised in the main introduction. The best way to help an audience sense a need is by asking questions around the theme of the central proposition in relation to the purpose of the sermon.

For instance, your sermon on Ephesians 4 could have the following need questions.

- How many of you would like to find out what is wrong with our church?
- How would you like to get our church to obey God's will?
- How many would care to find out how to grow our church to the maximum?
- Would you like to find out God's blueprint for building our congregation?

Most people would answer these questions affirmatively, truly desiring to find out what is wrong with their church and how to correct it.

If you are speaking on the Ephesians 6:10–12 passage, the need could be stated this way: "Today I am going to speak on how you can beat Satan at his own game in his own field." The need you raise relates to how believers can have consistent victory over the devil as he constantly seeks to derail us spiritually. In pinpointing the need, you are providing a reason for your audience to listen to your message.

Orient theme. The attention-getter and need-raiser ingredients of the main introduction will naturally be related to the theme of the CPS. That is, you should not raise a need about handling anger and then talk about the angelic hosts of heaven. In your main introduction, you will orient the audience to the theme that you are going to pursue. You may even express the whole central proposition of the sermon here if you are following a deductive form of the sermon.

On Ephesians 6:10–12 tell your audience you are going to speak on the theme, "Why sovereign strength is sufficient for your strategy against Satan."

State purpose. Since you have already written out the purpose bridge, state the purpose of the sermon. Tell the audience, "Today I want to. . . ." In the case of Ephesians 4, you could say, "Today I want to challenge each member of our church to become involved in putting God's plan into action." This purpose statement shows the destination of the sermon. A purpose statement invites the audience to travel along on the journey. People do not want to get on a bus that is not going anywhere! Just remember to get this purpose statement from step 4—the purpose bridge.

So these are the four ingredients or goals of the main introduction. Including all four will help you get and hold the attention of your audience.

Goals of an Effective Introduction

- To get the attention of the audience
- To raise a pertinent need
- To orient the audience to the theme
- To state the purpose of the sermon

The main introduction needs to be long enough to raise the need, orient the audience to the theme, and state the purpose. The amount of time will vary from sermon to sermon. Allow sufficient time to include the ingredients of a strong main introduction, but don't make it so long that your audience wishes that the conclusion of your main introduction is really the conclusion of the entire sermon.

Never start the main introduction with, "Last week we considered the text or the theme (from the previous passage); this week we will consider the next passage. . . ." This kind of review belongs in the pre-introduction at best (but that section must be brought to a discernible close before you start the main introduction). The review is better included in the sub-introduction when you set the scene. Your main introduction should refer only to this week's passage and sermon.

Sub-Introduction

The natural place for setting the background of the text is right after an effective introduction. I call this the "sub-introduction." Since you are not quite yet into the body of the sermon, this is a good time to set the historical or contextual background of the text. Do this only if it helps you accomplish the purpose of the sermon from step 4.

In the sub-introduction you could include matters such as:

- Announcing or reminding the audience which text you are considering, e.g., "Paul speaks about the issue of marrying unbelievers in 1 Corinthians 7. If you have not found the passage yet, would you please turn to it as we answer the question, Are unbelievers eligible as potential spouses if believers are not to be found?"
- Reviewing a particular sermon series, e.g., "We are in a series that looks at how Christians must relate to society. Today, we want to consider Galatians 6:10."
- Background to the text:

  —*historical* background of the text, e.g., "David wrote Psalm 51 after he sinned against God."

  —*textual* background of the text, e.g., "Revelation 2 through 3 contains seven letters to the churches of Asia. We are in letter number seven, the letter to the church in Laodicea."

  —*literary* background of a text, e.g., "Psalm 119 is an acrostic."

—*sermon series* background to a text, e.g., "Last week we studied about the unity of Christ's body in Ephesians 4:1–6. This week we are continuing our studies on Christ's body—how it can grow and function according to the divine blueprint."

- Previewing body structure, e.g., "Our text, Psalm 133, divides into a statement and two pictures. Verse 1 provides the thesis; verses 2 and 3 paint portraits of the thesis."

Finally, repeat the theme or the central proposition of the sermon.

Again, do not start with sub-introductory contents in the main introduction.

In appendix 10 I have given an illustration of a rather full introduction and sub-introduction that I used for the sermon on Revelation 4. There you will see the ingredients of an effective (not perfect!) introduction.

Body of the Sermon

Design Structure

Again, when we speak about design structure (relating to the whole sermon—introduction, body, and conclusion), we are taking into account the audience's inability to agree with or accept or apply the sermon. You need to think and work through the following questions: Why would they have difficulty in being persuaded concerning God's truth in this CPS? How should I design this sermon to accomplish the purpose of the sermon and present the central proposition of the sermon to make an impact on the lives of the people?

There is a range of people in your audience, and parts of your presentation need to address these varied people. Further, at different times of their lives (and even within a single sermon) people may assume different postures toward you. Sometimes your audience will consist of the majority of one kind of people. Each such group needs to be considered as you design your sermon. In relation to God, his Word, his people, and you, there are at least three possible stances that people maintain concerning the preaching event.

- The *I Don't Cares!* Some feel they should not be in the service in the first place. They are not hostile, but they really don't care about God and his Word. They are there because their parents or friends wanted them to come. Or they are there because going to church is what they do at this time of the week. The need you raise must be extremely effective at this point or you will lose the little interest you gained by getting up there.
- The *I Don't Knows!* Others in your audience do not know much about God, his Word, his people, and you. This is why your sermon needs good biblical content.
- The *I Don't Believes!* These people are somewhat doubtful of the truth of what you say or its applicability in daily life. They may apply a philosophical test to what you have to say: Is the truth coherent? Is the sermon consistent? They often use a pragmatic test on the sermon: Is the truth practical? Does it work? They may say, "Pastor, what you say sounds good from the pulpit, but it does not work in real life."

You may face combinations of these attitudes at different times during your message and sometimes from the same person. Think through how you should design the sermon to meet them at the level of their attitudes to take them to the level that God desires of them. An expositional ministry allows you to put a weekly dent in their apathy, passivity, ignorance, or hostility to equip them for godliness and service.

The fourth group of people consists of those who are easiest to address. They are eager and motivated to hear and do God's Word. They care, know, and believe. These challenge you to impact them with God's truth so that they can become godlier.

A variety of preaching audiences needs a variety of preaching approaches.[2] Appendix 8 has information on understanding your audience. Use the sociological and psychological indicators given there to design your sermon so that your audience will accept and obey its central proposition.

Body Structure

The structure of the body of the sermon will be similar (not identical) to the structure of the text. If your text had three main points, the body of your sermon will usually reflect that number—in contemporized and concrete terminology. If your structure had two subpoints under your first main point, so will your sermon's body.

Let's look at a diagram of this relationship.

Step 2 (Text)	Step 6 (Sermon)
1. Verses 1–3	*Introduction*
2. Verses 4–6	*Body*
3. Verses 7–8	1. Verses 1–3
	2. Verses 4–6
	3. Verses 7–8
	Conclusion

Thus the structure of the body of the sermon is dependent on the structure of the text.

Sometimes students ask if the sequence of the body of the sermon will be the same sequence as the text. Usually it is, but it depends on the design of the sermon. If the purpose (step 4) of the sermon is best accomplished by a rearrangement of the main points to make your point clear, you may preach verses 4 to 6 first, followed by verses 7 and 8 with verses 1 to 3 following. Notice, however, that the *segments* of the passage are kept together. That is, if you are preaching verses 1–8, you should not preach verses 4 and 5 as a single unit, giving verses 4 and 5 the same weight as verse 6, if verses 4 to 6 make a single unit. You must respect the divisions of the text. And most often your sermon will reflect the sequence of the text as well.

Consult appendix 9 on the elements of a competent outline. Briefly, your outline will exhibit the following characteristics.[3]

Unity—the sermon as a whole
Order—the parts of the sermon as they relate to the whole sermon
Proportion—appropriate lengths of the parts
Progress—how each major point moves the sermon forward

Every point of the outline, especially the main points and the first level of subpoints, will exhibit the features summarized in the phrase "SAVE (a) Point!" Each letter indicates what one must do to effectively present a point in expository preaching.

> *State* the point. To help the audience clearly hear the point you are making, use contemporary and concrete language.
>
> *Anchor* the point. Give authority to the point by anchoring it in the text.
>
> *Validate* the point. Explain why you have drawn this particular point from a text.
>
> *Explain* the point. Here you probe the meaning of the point. Use your study (step 1) to help with your explanation. Use an illustration to help the people understand this point as biblically elicited and referring to them. You may have heard of the "frame of reference" principle of communication. A speaker must utilize the audience's frame of reference to explain a point. Go from the known to the unknown, from what your audience understands to what you want them to grasp.
>
> *(a)pply* the point. Sometimes a point needs to be applied right here and now. At other times it needs to be explained but applied later. The application of a point depends on the design structure of the sermon and how you think the purpose of the sermon will be best accomplished. Later in this chapter we will deal more with how to make appropriate applications.

Generally, in a deductive sermon, or one in which each main point is self-contained, application is made at each major point. We preach the first point and then the application, the second point and then the application, and so on. In an inductive structure, or a sermon in which each main point builds to a climax or to the final central proposition of the sermon, your application may well be placed toward the end.

The deductive design is a simpler design to follow, and many sermons follow this design. Each main point (and perhaps the first level of subpoints) follows the SAVE (a) Point structure. An inductive design follows the SAVE format, but the application comes later. This is why I have the letter *a* in parentheses in SAVE (a) point.

The following chart shows the deductive and inductive designs. I am using a two-point textual structure (from step 2) translated into the design structure (step 6).

Deductive	Inductive
I. Introduction	I. Introduction
CPS fully stated	CPS partially introduced
II. Body	II. Body
A. S.A.V.E.	A. S.A.V.E.
(a)pplication	B. S.A.V.E.
B. S.A.V.E.	(a)pplication
(a)pplication	(may be placed here)
III. Conclusion	III. Conclusion
	(may include application)

Transitions

As you think through the outline of the body of the sermon and the major points, you will need appropriate transitions to relate each part of the outline to the theme or to the previous section. Transitions accomplish smoothness of thought and understanding. They serve as bridges between parts or movements of the sermon so that the audience doesn't have to leap across intellectual or psychological rivers. Transition statements guarantee that the audience will follow the progress of the sermon.

Solid transitions enable the preacher to:

- review the theme of the sermon without monotony
- progress without hurdles
- connect parts without confusion
- remember the sermon without rote memorization
- preserve the planned structure of the sermon

A proper transitional statement, then, checks and guarantees the sermon's unity, order, and progress.

Transitions Guarantee

Unity
Order
Progress

Using our bones metaphor, transitions show connections between big bones, between small bones, and between big bones and small bones.

Below are various kinds of transitions with examples. You will create these sentences according to your sermon structure (design structure and body structure).

- *Phrase Transitions.* Use conjunctions and coordinating phrases, such as *not only this but, in the next place, whereas, besides, on the contrary.*
- *Point Transitions.* Review a point before going on to the next one. There are many ways to do this:

    —*Chronological point transitions:* "The first point we considered was . . ." "We now turn to the second point."

    —*Logical point transitions:* Used in building an argument and often found in inductive designs.

    —*Metaphorical point transitions:* Use metaphors to represent the points. For example, you might try the building metaphor: "The foundation of our faith is . . . ; the superstructure is . . ." Or you might use the wheel metaphor: "The first spoke of the wheel was . . . ; the second spoke is . . ."

    —*Psychological point transitions:* Use associations already in the mind of the audience instead of chronological or logical terms: "We have seen that . . . ; now, we need to see . . ."
- *Physical Transitions.* You can also indicate transitions between points and subpoints by gesture, posture, or position. You may use your fingers or even the place where you stand at certain segments of the sermon to show transition. We will be dealing more with physical delivery issues in step 7.

Application

Biblical exposition without application leads to spiritual consti-
pation. There is no point in being academically accurate if the information does not transform your hearers. The application is when
you move your audience from just receiving revelation to implementation of God's truth. The apostle Paul often turns to application in his epistles as he changes from making assertions (Greek,
indicative mood) to commands (Greek, imperative mood). Appropriate application must be customized and made concrete for your
audience.

- *Customized.* We have noted before how the same CPS will apply
  to different audiences in different ways. The audience is the
  variable. Thus there are spiritual, cultural, economic, and envi-
  ronmental variables. We must customize and fit the application to the audience. The process will have already begun in
  step 1 (see pages 47–49) and crystallizes in step 4 when you put
  together the purpose of the sermon. Now in the application
  you cross another threshold. You express God's claim in the
  present tense. It is not enough to tell your audience that God
  wants them to be holy. You must communicate what being holy
  looks like in their lives today.
- *Concrete.* The application must be concrete. If your application is abstract, your audience will tend to think about the
  words you said rather than how those words should affect their
  lives. Be specific about God's expectations of your people. It is
  not enough to tell them that God wants them to be holy. You
  must give specific examples of holiness that will be relevant to
  their situation today.

In order to customize your application and make it concrete, you
need to look for homiletical correlation or links between the central proposition of the text (not just the sermon) and your audience.
(For guidance on careful application of narrative texts, see appendix 6.) These links are theological and spiritual. Using illustrations
from the Revelation 4 passage we used earlier, I will list here the

kinds of correlations I seek theologically and spiritually in the pursuit of contemporization.

The CPT I developed in step 3 for Revelation 4:1–11 was: "The exclusive throne right of God to rule over the affairs of history is recognized by the residents of heaven." Theological and spiritual links can connect my audience to the CPT.

- *Theological Links.*
  —The nature of God and his works. We recognize that God rules and must be God.
  —The nature of God's people. We can see community or ecclesiological links: e.g., the twenty-four elders and redeemed people.
  —The nature of creation/creatures. The angels worship God; so must we.
- *Spiritual Links.* Existential, dynamic, and personal aspects of relationships to God. I ask, What about the first audience? Did anyone then experience the antichrist spirit of self-focused sovereignty? What issue was John addressing? What did they make of this passage? Ask the following questions about the nature of persons then and now.
  —How are we like them? We too belong to God and must worship.
  —How are we unlike them? We are not residents of heaven. (You would have to show why our not being like heaven's residents does not excuse us from the kind of worship they give to God.)
  —How should we be like them? In worship.
  —How should we be unlike them? Some were tempted to give up on the God who rules over history as life got difficult under Antichrist. (You could have pursued this aspect of the text and come up with a totally different purpose than the one I came up with. I wanted to challenge each believer to relinquish throne rights to his or her life.)

From a panorama of applicational possibilities for homiletical correlations, I selected the particular application that could be customized and made concrete according to the purpose of the sermon. Before choosing application, I went back to the CPT so that I would be faithful to the text rather than impose my application whims on my audience.

Locating Application

Again, you may make applications in the body of the sermon (in a deductive design structure) or toward the end of the sermon (in an inductive design structure). You can locate the application when and where it is necessary, taking into consideration the following factors: the design structure of the sermon, the body structure of the sermon, the purpose of the sermon, and the central proposition of the sermon. Perhaps you are exploring one part of the central proposition in a particular segment of the sermon. Seize the moment for application at that time. If your application should come at the end of the sermon, do not view it as a mere footnote to the "real stuff" that you have already given. The application should not be an appendix to the sermon. It must be given adequate time and place.

Developing Application

By the end of the sermon the audience must have the answers to three important questions:

What did the preacher speak about?
So what difference does or should it make?
Now what do I do with God's claims in this sermon?

The central proposition of the sermon and the body of the sermon should answer the what question (What did the preacher speak about?). The application and the stylized CPS address the so what (So what difference does it make?). The application will also focus on the now what (Now what do I do?) question.

The purpose you developed in step 4 will help you see what application you should make. Your purpose bridge addressed the question. On the basis of the central proposition of the text, what does God want my audience to understand and obey? The purpose you wrote out would have contained the word *to* followed by an explicit, compelling action verb. (In grammar this is called an infinitive.) Half seriously, let me list a few purpose verbs beginning with the letter *C:* To coax, cheer, champion, confront, convince, convict, challenge, correct, comfort, call. (But do not attempt to convert, for this is the responsibility of the Holy Spirit; nor to coerce, for even God does not do that!)

From the purpose statement, which begins with the infinitive and is based on the CPT, write out answers to the "so what" and "now what" questions as resources for application. In fact, use a separate sheet of paper for the answers to each of these questions. You can throw out inappropriate and extraneous applications later.

A sermon carries two types of application:[4]

1. Tension and complication in becoming or being a Christian
   • Spiritual tensions or spiritual needs
   • Intellectual tensions or theological/philosophical needs
   • Emotional tensions or relational/psychological needs
   • Physical and other existential tensions or survival needs
2. Solution and resolution to the tension

What tension should you evoke in your introductory need and expect the sermon to answer? Well, in textual exposition, the framework of the tensions arises from the CPT. The answers and application of the solution come from the correlation of the central proposition of the sermon to life through the purpose bridge. Or to put it another way:

• The "what" comes from the authority of Scripture culminating in the central proposition of the text.
• The "so what" comes from the authority of life, with the purpose bridge drawn from the central proposition of the text, yielding the central proposition of the sermon.
• The "now what" comes from the authority of the preacher as he incarnates and contextualizes the specific expectations of God in a contemporary setting.[5]

There are five arenas of life where truth must apply (so what?) and be specified (now what?). Think through these five arenas in developing your applications to discover how God's truth will make a difference and how it will call his people to obedience.

Application Arenas of Life

What kind of a person does God want us to become in:

1. Personal life
2. Home life
3. Work or study life
4. Church life
5. Community life

Before I spoke at a church in San Antonio, Texas, the pastor ushered me into his study. On the wall over his desk he had a few questions he asked concerning every sermon he preached. I found them helpful and share them with you:

Application Avenues in Life

How should this truth affect our
1. Attitudes—toward God, others, circumstances
2. Knowledge of God
3. Behavior—habits to develop, habits to change, habits to confirm
4. Relationships—Where do I need to forgive, seek forgiveness, encourage, rebuke, submit, lead?
5. Motives—Am I doing right for the wrong reasons?
6. Values and priorities—Who or what comes first? Who or what should?
7. Character

Mix these application avenues with the application arenas and come up with plans of response and action for you and your congregation.

Sermon Development with Application

I will illustrate the sermon movements toward application here, using a text from Matthew. The biblical text follows.

Forgiveness Frees!
Matthew 18:21–35

²¹Then Peter came and said to Him, "Lord how often shall my brother sin against me and I forgive him? Up to seven times?"

²²Jesus said to him, "I do not say to you, up to seven times, but up to seventy times seven.

²³"For this reason the kingdom of heaven may be compared to a certain king who wished to settle accounts with his slaves.

²⁴"And when he had begun to settle them, there was brought to him one who owed him ten thousand talents.

²⁵"But since he did not have the means to repay, his lord commanded him to be sold, along with his wife and children and all that he had, and repayment to be made.

²⁶"The slave therefore falling down, prostrated himself before him, saying, 'Have patience with me, and I will repay you everything.'

²⁷"And the lord of that slave felt compassion and released him and forgave him the debt.

²⁸"But that slave went out and found one of his fellow-slaves who owed him a hundred denarii, and he seized him and began to choke him, saying, 'Pay back what you owe.'

²⁹"So his fellow-slave fell down and began to entreat him, saying, 'Have patience with me and I will repay you.'

³⁰"He was unwilling however, but went and threw him in prison until he should pay back what was owed.

³¹"So when his fellow-slaves saw what had happened, they were deeply grieved and came and reported to their lord all that had happened.

³²"Then summoning him, his lord said to him, 'You wicked slave, I forgave you all that debt because you entreated me.

³³'Should you not also have had mercy on your fellow-slave, even as I had mercy on you?'

³⁴"And his lord, moved with anger, handed him over to the torturers until he should repay all that was owed him.

³⁵"So shall My heavenly Father also do to you, if each of you does not forgive his brother from your heart."

Step 3: CPT—The forgiven slave's unwillingness to forgive his debtor resulted in imprisonment.

Step 4: My purpose is to confront unforgiveness in the lives of forgiven people.

Step 5: An initial raw CPS may look like this:

Theme: What happens if you don't forgive?

Thrust: You will not enjoy your forgiveness and be imprisoned in unforgiveness.

After some thought and work in contemporization, I came up with a CPS based on the CPT and processed through my purpose. I wanted something for my audience to remember each time they were unforgiving. This is my CPS: *"Forgiveness frees you up; unforgiveness locks you in."*

Step 6: So far in this chapter we have worked on design structure, introduction, and body structure, including the transitions and applications of the sermon.

Introduction. Here I will speak about unforgiveness in the lives of my listeners. Where might they withhold forgiveness and hold on to anger—against friends, bosses, family members, spouses, parents?

By the time I finish with the introduction, my audience will sense the tension of unforgiveness. I will attempt to help them think through areas of bitterness. I will ask the question, "How many times should I forgive someone who does the same thing over and over again to me?"

Transition Statement: Peter asked Jesus the same question (v. 21).

Sub-Introduction: I use the text to set the context (vv. 21–22).

Body Structure: (not design structure now)

  I. Forgiveness frees you up (vv. 21–27)
  II. Unforgiveness locks you in (vv. 28–35)

Application. Since my purpose is to confront unforgiveness in the lives of my audience, my main emphasis will not be "Forgiveness frees you up." I will mention that they are sitting in the audience as forgiven people. I will speak about the enormous, unpayable debt we owed God and how we were forgiven like the slave on that day. Now, if my purpose is to remind believers of God's great forgiveness, I should pursue the "so what" and "now what" in reference to God's great forgiveness.

My purpose, however, is to confront unforgiveness in my audience. Thus I will spend a lot more application time on point II. In this case, the text itself has the "so what" answered. If God has forgiven you, the text beckons you to become a forgiving person.

When I considered the three questions a sermon must answer in relation to this text, I found the following.

- *What?* (What truth will I speak about?) Forgiveness frees; unforgiveness freezes!
- *So What?* (What difference should the truth make?) You must forgive your debtor. Perhaps your husband has been negligent or unfaithful to you. Perhaps your wife has not been respectful at home. Perhaps a friend has betrayed you. I will go through such categories in my introduction to the sermon.
- *Now What?* (How should you obey the truth?) How will you forgive? I will have several suggestions for my people. First, refocus on God's forgiveness and compare it with what your offender has done against you. Who has committed the greater wrong? If you have been forgiven of an unpayable debt, what must you do with a payable debt? Second, give up any thought of the right to take revenge. Third, redistribute culpability in the offense. The entire blame cannot be laid on your debtor. Fourth, seek overt ways in which you can demonstrate forgiveness.

Expect some excuses or at least questions about your application. Because people (myself included) like to apply truth to someone else rather than to themselves, you will have to anticipate some of the objections they may have toward your sermon. One of my definitions of an effective sermon includes the provision for answers to (m)any questions people may have.

Here are some questions about unforgiveness I expect my audience will have. Most of them will be "I don't believes" (see page 108), and my hearers will want to know how the truth of my sermon works for them (the pragmatic test). I attempt to prepare answers to their questions.

- What if he does not know that he has offended me?

- Will my constant forgiveness not be too indulgent? For example, is it not unwise to allow a debtor to keep borrowing money from me?
- What if the relationship is irretrievable—a former spouse who has remarried?
- What if the offender is dead?

Remember, for the people, your sermon is like the viewfinder in a single-lens reflex camera. People may begin to understand a general idea of God's claim from the body of your sermon, but application takes the haziness of an image and brings it into sharp focus for obedience.

Illustrations

The impact of a sermon is always connected to the illustrations in it. This is true all over the world. Good communicators use many effective illustrations. Think of all the good preachers you have heard, starting with the Lord Jesus. Without exception, they are excellent storytellers. Why? Because stories, or illustrations, comply with the most basic principle of communication. They take the listener from the known to the unknown.

The Value of Illustrations

The purpose of illustrations is to illustrate. It is wrong to use illustrations with the purpose of lengthening the sermon. Illustrations are used to add light, not length. They make the material understandable, but they should not be the focal point of your sermon. Illustrations are not used to entertain (though they may carry some entertainment value); they are to help the audience understand the content or the claims of what is being illustrated. When we find a powerful illustration, we are sometimes tempted to try to make the sermon fit it. The sermon then takes on the direction of the illustration, and the audience leaves remembering the illustration more than the point the illustration was highlighting. Here is another reason why your purpose bridge is extremely critical. The purpose bridge will help screen out (and screen in) the right illustrations. Illustrations should not be the focus of your sermons. Though they are eminently preachable, you are not in a pulpit to preach an illustration. You are there to preach the Bible through many effective means, including illustrations.

A good communicator will use illustrations, but he or she must use them at the right places, at the right times, and for the right purpose.

Let me suggest several benefits of using illustrations.

Illustrations Help Avoid

- misunderstanding
- distraction
- neglect
- monotony
- apathy

• *Avoid misunderstanding.* Illustrations illuminate. They cast light on the concepts and the direction of the sermon. They help people understand and help the preacher explain himself. In a video production, bright lights are turned on to illuminate the details of the subject to be captured on film. Similarly, illustrations light up the details of the sermon in the minds of the hearers. You can't make good videos in the dark.

• *Avoid tedium and distraction.* If you use the sermonic system outlined in this book, you will accumulate many particulars to give your people. After exegetical study of the Scriptures, you may be tempted to dump truthful minutiae and exegetical trivia on a rather unprepared audience. Unfortunately, people may get bored with truth, especially if it is minutiae with little clear relevance to the main points of your sermon. Your responsibility is to lighten what would be a burdensome weight of your sermon by illustrating all the necessary details. Your illustrations can arouse and maintain interest during the sermon.

• *Avoid neglect.* Good illustrations not only arouse interest but encourage long-term retention. Illustrations are like photographs that evoke memories of long-ago events. Illustrations also stir the imagination as people make intellectual and psychological associations with what they already know. In this way, they keep hearing the sermon in their minds, even after the service is over. Illustrations help truth go into automatic pilot as people travel their spiritual journeys.

• *Avoid monotonous content and argument.* All preachers get stuck in modes of thinking and preaching they have found to be successful. Unless you are naturally creative, you will need to work at communicating in an interesting manner. One way to be liberated from the safety of the familiar is to sprinkle your sermons with a variety of illustrations. This demands that you broaden your style of thinking and talking. A variety of illustrations will appeal to a variety of hearers. Young people will especially appreciate good illustrations. When children (not my own!) compliment one of my sermons, they usually refer to my stories. The stories kept them listening.

• *Avoid apathy.* I used the camera illustration to show how application focuses the sermon. Often in application you will employ illustrations to challenge people to action. Illustrations during application or at the conclusion actually demonstrate the real-life workability of the sermon. They keep people from excusing themselves from obedience.

The Search for Illustrations

If you look and pray for appropriate illustrations during sermon preparation, God will provide them. You will find the best illustrations when you are thinking about what you want to illustrate. Your mind will be attuned to the precise point and your eyes engaged in finding illustrations for the point.

The only one way to find illustrations is to observe life. Beecher uses biblical words to tell preachers how to find illustrations: "Having eyes, you must see; having ears, you must hear; and having a heart, you must understand."[6] And then you must invent and innovate, using your imagination to translate an event to fit what you want. You must observe, observe, observe!

There are four sources of illustrations.

Sources of Illustrations

Your life
Someone else's life
Everyone's life
No one's life

Your personal life is a splendid source of illustrations, and they are often your best illustrations because you know them so well. Never apologize for personal illustrations, but try not to be the hero of the story every time.

You could illustrate from someone else's experience—someone in the audience, in Scripture, in history, or in literature. Beware of giving out confidential information. If you are using history to illustrate, be sure that your people know the context of the story. That is, don't use in India an illustration from the American Civil War without adequate explanation. If you are an erudite scholar and want to quote from literary classics, remember that your audience may not be familiar with them. The Greek classics of Homer or Aristotle and the Reformation classics of Luther or Calvin may be boring to those who have no background in Western culture.

You may also illustrate from everyone's experience. For instance, you could illustrate from a triumph or a tragedy that has affected everyone in your audience. Perhaps all of them can connect with an earthquake or a plane crash or an election that has occurred.

If you are innovative and are blessed with an active imagination, you could create stories that no one has experienced but that illuminate the point. These are not false stories but fiction (which has no relation to the question of truth). For example, you could invent a conversation between the angel who announced Jesus' birth and the shepherds.

The Use of Illustrations

To properly use an illustration, the point you are illustrating must precede and succeed the illustration. This enables people to comprehend and recollect (then and later) the point you are making. The sequence of the illustration will look like this:

How to Use an Illustration

1. Make the point
2. Transition to illustration
3. Illustrate the point
4. Transition to audience
5. Restate/review the point

Here is the illustration sequence for a point I make on Psalm 133.

1. *The point.* When we are focused on a common purpose outside of us, there is unity.

2. *Transition to illustration.* We find this truth illustrated in how . . .

3. *Illustration.* Alaskan horses and donkeys encounter the hostility of wild hyenas in similar ways. When attacked, the horses form a circle with their heads to the inside, feet to the outside, and kick their enemies away. The donkeys form a circle too, with their feet to the inside, heads to the outside, and kick themselves to death.

4. *Transition to audience.*[7] We must be like Alaskan horses focusing on defeating the enemy rather than like those donkeys kicking themselves to death.

5. *Restate or review the point.* Unity, then, is found when we focus on a common purpose outside of us.

We now come to the issue of how often to use illustrations and how many to use. The basic challenge is to use as many illustrations as are needed to accomplish the purpose of the sermon. We never have enough time for all the illustrations (or even the fruits of our study) we would like to include, however. Therefore, we need to make some adjustments.

Where should you use illustrations? All the bare and boring regions of your sermon need illustrations. Some regions that always need illustrations are:

- the introduction, as you get the attention of your audience and raise the need
- each *major* point—I often attempt to insert mini-illustrations at the sublevel of points as well
- the conclusion, as you bring the sermon to a close

Think through the body of your sermon and ask the following questions to see where you need illustrations.[8]

- *The correlation question.* What illustration will meet the need for additional explanation of a particular section? If my point is "The Lord Jesus is with you always," it needs explanation. People may ask the following question: "If we can't see him, how do we know he is with us?" The question requires an illustration. We can use one from travel. Jesus is always with us like the unseen captain of the plane or ship who is with us throughout our journey.
- *The credibility question.* What illustration (or part of it) will help the audience see, believe, and accept the truth of my point? For example, I could use the illustration of how I was once on a storm-stricken boat that was maneuvered to safety by an unseen captain.
- *The claim question.* What illustration will help the audience explore the implication and application of the point to their lives? For example, my worrying while on the boat was useless since it did not help or hinder the skill of the captain or the safety of the boat.

There are many kinds of illustrations, and different cultures will prefer some kinds over others. "One-liners" without context will not work in some cultures. What is humorous to one audience may not be so to another audience. Also, some audiences are able to handle lengthy times of abstract speech while others are not. Anecdotes seem to be universally preferred, but you should adjust your stories to meet the needs of your particular audience.

In all of this, be sensitive to the audience's need for illustrations, their learning habits, and the local culture's way of narrating events while communicating truth. Also, when thinking through the need and the kind of illustration you must incorporate into your sermon, ask this question: What must I illustrate in the text to accomplish my purpose within my audience's frame of reference? What illustration will take them from known truth to unknown truth?

The Conclusion[9]

A conclusion completes the sermon. It integrates varied strands, reviews the central proposition of the sermon, resolves earlier irresolution, and invites the audience to obedience.

The conclusion will contain application. If application was not sprinkled through the body of the sermon, the conclusion must provide for application time.

The conclusion is the final movement of the sermon, so it crescendos to a climax. The preacher repeats or restates the central proposition to refocus the thoughts of the audience on what God expects of them. The conclusion will evidence two features, cohesion and resolution. *Cohesion:* The audience now hears in concise statements all the important points of the sermon. *Resolution:* The audience now has the feeling that the destination set out in the purpose during the introduction has been reached.[10]

Faulty Conclusions

Faulty conclusions are notoriously discouraging. Here are some ways to prevent them.

- Don't simply stop. How would you feel if just the first three lines of a favorite song were played and the musician quit?
- Don't give false cues. Some preachers close their Bibles long before they are finished. The audience sees this merciful gesture and wonders why the preacher is still going strong five minutes later. Some preachers say, "lastly," and last a long while. That word was a false cue.
- Don't try multiple conclusions. How would you like a pilot who keeps landing and taking off, never stopping at your destination?
- Don't introduce fresh thoughts in the conclusion.
- Don't construct a conclusion that is longer than the sermon.
- Don't give your conclusion before you get to the conclusion. If you do this, the audience may leave the room emotionally before you are finished.

- Don't develop "delivery droopiness" during the conclusion. Your conclusion is not ancillary, a footnote to the sermon. It is an integral part of the sermon. If your conclusion sounds unimportant, your audience will not give you the attention needed.

Skillful Conclusions

Here are some ideas for how to skillfully conclude a sermon.

- A clear statement of the central proposition along with a summarization of the main points is acceptable.
- Applications and implications woven with personal strategies for obedience are even more effective.
- A single-sentence affirmation of the truth, a contemporized and easily remembered version of the central proposition, is very good.
- A final story, which may illustrate the central proposition of the message (or the last point of the body), is useful if it meets the three criteria for illustrations: correlation, credibility, and claim.

If you have designed your application to be included in the latter part of the sermon, think through the issues of application mentioned earlier (for example, the "so what?" and "now what?" questions) to make your conclusion have impact.

What should you expect from your audience upon your conclusion? The best outcome would be a decision to put your final appeal into practice combined with creative ways to accomplish the character/conduct change you solicited. To use G. Campbell Morgan's phrase, an impacting conclusion "storms the citadel of the will." Go, storm your hearers' wills!

7

PREACH THE SERMON

The "Flesh" of the Sermon

Step 7: Preach the Sermon
Step 6: Structure the Sermon
Step 5: The Central Proposition of the Sermon
Step 4: The Purpose Bridge
Step 3: The Central Proposition of the Text
Step 2: Structure the Text
Step 1: Study the Text

We now come to putting the final touches on the sermon sculpture that you have created from Scripture. Writing and preaching the sermon finishes the Scripture Sculpture process. To preach the sermon well, I recommend that you write it out first. Writing helps put the final touches on the sermon. Then prepare yourself for delivering the sermon.

Writing the Sermon	Preaching the Sermon
Think about	
Sermon content	Preacher's style
Sermon design	Preacher's delivery

Writing the Sermon

Almost all of the work of the sermon has been done. Now you will put it on paper.

In seminary, when I was first asked to write my sermon, I experienced an internal reaction of sorts (not the best sort!). I had been preaching for many years and did not think that I needed to put my sermon in writing. Such a mundane procedure, I thought, would rob the spontaneity from my sermons. Further, my professors legislated that I preach without notes. This too I considered an encroachment on a preaching style developed through the years. But I decided to submit to professorial authority with explicit prescience that I would go back to spontaneous preaching with sparse notes after graduation. After all, what is the use of preaching without notes if you have prepared the sermon so thoroughly? And what is the use of writing full manuscripts if you don't take them to the pulpit?

After that preaching class I had to admit, rather sheepishly, that I had had a massive change of perspective and practice about using notes while preaching. Now I am glad to admit, somewhat boldly, that I have not used notes in the pulpit since that class. I do not need them after going through the rigor of the preaching regimen. That doesn't mean that I don't have notes. I have a full manuscript of every sermon I have preached. Indeed, the farther I depart from textual exposition, the more I become dependent on notes.

Write out every word you intend to preach in the way you intend to preach it. Notice that I said, "Write out every word you *intend* to preach." This may not be what actually happens in the pulpit. The Holy Spirit may change what you say. He has the right to intrude spontaneously. He is active in the whole sermon-making process—from the beginning when you committed your study time to him, to the end when you invite people to obey God's Word.

Writing out the manuscript has several advantages:

- You can actually see the development of the sermon, which may help you to enhance it.

- You can internalize (not memorize) the sermon *before* you preach it if it is on paper.
- You can improve the sermon as you become aware of new or better information.
- Your sermon manuscript will reveal areas that need to be reinforced with illustrations, transitions, and applications. You can also remove any material that is irrelevant or unclear.
- You will have some idea of how long the sermon will take and will be able to control its length. Experience will tell you how long it takes to preach through a page of sermon material. If it takes you five minutes to preach a page, an eight-page manuscript will take you about forty minutes to preach.
- Your exposure to the manuscript will jog your memory when you are in the pulpit. You will not need to take your manuscript or any notes to the pulpit. Once you have gone through the Scripture Sculpture process, you will know your material so well that the biblical text will provide memory clues to the manuscript you have prepared.
- You can preach the sermon again without leaving out anything important (though you will have to rework it to suit another audience). If you do not write out your sermon, you will never preach the same sermon again.
- You will have a record of illustrations you have already used so that you can avoid repeating them.
- You may want to publish your sermons in book form. In any case, you will have a permanent record of the sermon for later use.

There is no such thing as good preaching without preparation. There is, however, such a thing as good preaching without notes. Those who consistently preach extemporaneously may succumb to any momentary inspiration (often under the guise of spontaneity), lack variety in style, and repeat similar themes and illustrations because they have not prepared or planned their sermons. Except in the most unusual of circumstances, please do not attempt extemporaneous preaching if you want to feed your people a good, steady diet of God's Word.[1]

Language and Style

Aristotle said in *Rhetoric*, "It is not enough to know what to say; one must also know how to say it." *Style* has to do with using language to effectively communicate what you know you must say. In some parts of the world, *style* means "showing off" and relates to personal pride. In communication, style refers to the choice and use of language that gives form to our thoughts.

The question is not whether one has style in communication, for everyone has a style of communication. The question is whether one's style has impact or not. Many books have been written on this subject from Christian and non-Christian experts in public speaking.[2] There are many cultural angles to style (and delivery) as well. Some generic comments on style may be made with their application to a local congregation dependent on the preacher's personality, temperament, skill, and imagination.[3]

Use words (and sentences) that are clear and concrete. For instance, don't use words in your CPS that can carry several meanings. If a word has a double meaning, your audience may choose the wrong one. Clear words are neither abstract nor ambiguous. They are usually short, simple, and specific.

Use words that are evocative and sensuous. Your words must appeal to the senses. You want your audience to see, hear, touch, taste, smell, and even feel your image-laden words. Your words need to be more than sounds emanating from a voice box. Talk in pictures. Instead of saying "personal faith without public works is useless," say, "personal faith without public works is as useless as a coat hanger without a hook." The words we choose can also evoke feelings of joy, freedom, calm, anger, tension, guilt, or whatever is appropriate to the purpose of the sermon.

Image-Laden Words

(Word Choice)
Are my words clear and concrete?
Are my words evocative and sensuous?

To grow in this aspect of sermon preparation, you must know your audience. Remember, you are writing your sermon for them. Think through their experiences to determine what will help you communicate with power. Use terminology they know and with which you are comfortable. Stay away from clichés, which are too familiar to have impact. Ask yourself what you want your audience to hear from your sermon and how you want them to hear it. Then develop your style accordingly. Let your sermon throb with color, sound, taste, odor, and feel. If you don't fire up your sermon with images, your sermon should be set on fire.

As you write your sermon, use this test question for style. Is it understandable and interesting? Work on the words, the sentences, and the paragraphs, rewriting, reworking, and rewording until it is both understandable and interesting.

What about humor in the pulpit? If you have a humorous temperament, use humor to communicate wisdom. This is how humor is used in Scripture. Do not use humor to simply fill time or entertain or enhance your reputation. I know one priest in South Asia who is so humorous that people actually start laughing before he utters the first syllable. That is similar to what we expect of circus clowns whether or not they are funny. This is inappropriate in the pulpit.

Humor can be extremely effective, however, in gaining credibility for the preacher in showing his personal foibles, for maintaining interest and creating expectation throughout the sermon, for disarming his hearers' defensiveness, and for illuminating the truth.

Style, then, is what brings your sermon to life with flesh and bones and sweat.

Sequence and Components

Follow step 6, "Structure the Sermon," carefully in writing out the sermon. Here is a review of the sequence and components.

Title

The title is the identity of the sermon. It should be contemporary, accurate, clear, and short.

Text

The text could be declared and/or read in one of many places, as was pointed out in step 6.

Pre-Introduction

The transition from your pre-introductory comments to the sermon is made by pause, prayer, reading of text, or some other signal to the audience that you are about to begin the sermon. You will not write out the pre-introduction, but you must plan for it.

Introduction

The introduction should get attention, raise need, orient the theme, state the purpose. The central proposition of the sermon is placed at the end of the introduction if it is a deductive sermon; in an inductive sermon, only your theme will be stated in the introduction.

Sub-Introduction

Give background and context of the text. Introduce the main sections of the sermon or just the first main section. The CPS or even the CPT could be stated or repeated here.

Body of the Sermon

Based on the outline in step 6 (see page 99), here are some things to remember as you write the body of your sermon.

I. First Main Section
   State the main point of this section in a complete sentence. Remember SAVE (a) Point! STATE it, ANCHOR it, VALIDATE it, EXPLAIN it, and possibly *apply* it.
   Be sure to introduce the subsections of this main point.
   A. First subpoint of first main point
      You may want to introduce the sub-subsections of this subsection.
      1. First sub-subsection
      2. Second sub-subsection
         You may want to review the sub-subsections before going on to the second subsection.
   B. Second subsection

After covering all the subsections of this point, review the CPS (in a deductive sermon) or the theme (in an inductive sermon) or the preceding subsections and the first main section. Then transition to the second main section.

Be sure to have one solid illustration for the first main section:

Make the point
Transition to illustration
Illustrate the point
Transition to audience
Restate/review the point

In a deductive sermon, make application of the first main point here. It should be a customized and concrete application.

You will follow the same structure for each section of your sermon.

At the end of the last main section, fully state the CPS. (It is repeated here for emphasis and review in a deductive sermon.) A customized and concrete application is placed here in the inductive sermon.

Conclusion

Use the conclusion to make application, restate the CPS, summarize, and bring the sermon to an impressive climax.

Internalizing the Sermon

Having written out the sermon, you will have to internalize (not memorize) it. The good thing is that, since you shaped the sermon from the very beginning, it is already a part of your soul. Your text and preparation will act as memory clues in the pulpit. You will not need to memorize the sermon word for word, though you may need to work on remembering certain illustrations and you may want to practice your style of delivery of some sections at least early in your preaching career. For instance, if you are attempting to include a humorous anecdote, you need to learn how to tell it. Otherwise your audience will be laughing at you rather than with you. If you desire to cite a quotation and have not been able to memorize it, put it on a small piece of paper and read from it during the sermon.

Most of the sermon, however, you will not need to memorize. I suggest that you put the entire sermon—points, illustrations, and all—on half sheets of paper while studying your sermon for delivery.[4] My own mnemonic habits require that I write out the outline by hand as I study my sermon. I use two colors on this half-page outline—blue or black for the main points and subpoints and red for the illustrations. A lack of red in any part of the outline alerts me to check the need for an illustration and to include it as necessary. This outline follows the sermon structure given earlier in this chapter.

Francis Bacon said, "Reading maketh a full man; conference a ready man; writing an exact man." I cherish the notion that some-day preachers will be called "exact men"!

Preaching the Sermon

You have prepared the sermon through six and a half stages. You have written out the sermon for internalization, storage, and future reference. We now come to the actual delivery of the sermon.

My limited experience shows that non-Western speakers have distinct advantages in speech delivery over their Western counter-parts. People growing up in these story- and speech-oriented cultures have had their delivery skills strengthened from childhood. Even in personal conversation, a good amount of physical energy is expended. In cultures affected by a Greek philosophical bias tending to the intellect, however, the emphasis is often on the quality of the content rather than its delivery. Of course, there are exceptions to this general observation.

Nonverbal Communication

Delivery relates to the preacher—his face, gestures, and voice. These are called nonverbal media of communication. The use of the face, gestures, and voice sometimes has more impact than the content of what you have to say. I once had lunch with a friend who, while conversing (reasonably intelligently) with me, kept looking at his watch. What aspect of his communication do you think was more powerful? Nonverbal media should be used very skillfully and appropriately. Your body talks along with your mouth, and there needs to be parity between them.

These nonverbal media communicate your enthusiasm for the sermon, enhance your presence on the pulpit, and actually create a whole emotional environment for your sermon. That is, your sermon may be brilliant, but if you do not use nonverbal media skillfully and appropriately, they can veto what you have to say.[5]

Your Face

I realize that some have advantages over others in this area, but I find that I do not need to be discouraged about such a disadvantage in the pulpit. People are not only willing to put up with my face but actually watch my face for how I feel about the sermon, myself, and them. Some studies say that more than half of a speaker's believability comes from the facial aspects of communication.

Eye contact with your audience in culturally appropriate ways must be maintained as much as possible. I have a friend who speaks to an invisible second balcony and another friend who looks out the side windows, which are not there. I have on occasion moved my head from side to side as though I were watching a tennis match. We need to correct these distracting habits. Look directly at your audience. If you have a large audience, pick one on each side, one in the front, and one at the back and speak to these people, personally.

Smile occasionally. It is appropriate to smile in the pulpit as long as you don't look like you're in a toothpaste commercial. Go ahead and smile when it is normal to your disposition, natural to your content, and appropriate to your culture. You have to choose something between a hellish look and a heavenly look in the pulpit. Was it Spurgeon who said something like, "When you speak about heaven, let your face shine; when you speak about hell, your normal face would do"?

People can tell the difference between a shining face and an angry face, a joyous face and a sorrowful face, an enthusiastic face and a boring face.

Your Gestures

Just like your face, your body talks. It will add to or subtract from your verbal communication.

There are three possible relationships between your body and your words:

- *Inaction.* The body just comes along for the sermon event. Like resurrected Lazarus emerging from the tomb wrapped in grave cloths, your body is stifled or disabled.

- *Overaction and wrong action.* Either of these are distracting. Your gestures, posture, and movement should not call attention to what you are doing. Then your body becomes the main focus of the audience's attention. When I was a teenager I used to sit at the side of the pulpit in our church and count the number of times my pastor bent his legs up to knee level. Another preacher had itching ears and would put his little finger into his ear during the sermon. Some remind me of Paul's analogy of a boxer who fights and beats the air. Don't develop distracting mannerisms, such as playing with the keys in your pocket or constantly adjusting your glasses.

- *Appropriate action.* Your whole body should be natural as you communicate, and your gestures should give the same message as your words. For example, do not point down while referring to heaven. Don't put up three fingers for your second point. Your body language can effectively reinforce your points: The pointing finger, the querying eyebrows, the wide arms, the clenched fist, the open palms, and many others, if done naturally and at appropriate places in your sermon, can be assets to your presentation.

I find some students to be full of energy at home (for instance, at their child's birthday party), but they are transformed into Egyptian mummies in the pulpit. Your whole body is at your disposal to use to enhance your verbal material. It is interesting that it takes the same amount of psychological and physical energy to be inhibited as it takes to be free in the pulpit.

Nervousness is okay. It is a reminder of your frailty and the need for dependence on the Holy Spirit. If the nervousness relates to how well you are going to perform, then it is an unholy nervousness. Your identity cannot be defined by how well you preach from the pulpit. If preaching provides the grid for your self-identity, I guarantee you are destined for depression. Direct your nervousness toward trust and openness to God, the Holy Spirit. Use it to trigger further reliance on the power of the Holy Spirit and the Word to free you from self-imposed or external constrictions as you minister to his people.

Use gestures skillfully and appropriately. Do what is natural for you while being sensitive to your culture in adopting proper gestures. Ask someone to videotape you while you are preaching, so you can evaluate your style and eliminate unskillful and inappropriate gestures. They can erase the tape later!

Your Voice

Since the tone of your voice communicates more than the content of your talk, it is essential to use your voice effectively. You must find the appropriate pitch and quality and develop variety in speed and volume.

Pitch

Is your voice too deep or too high?

Do you vary your pitch?

Are you able to inflect your voice to communicate feelings such as joy, urgency, command, or affirmation?

Quality

Does your voice have a nasal sound?

Does your voice have a harsh sound?

Do you sound smooth and relaxed?

Articulation and pronunciation[6]

Do you speak clearly and carefully?

Do you pronounce words in an understandable manner? Check a dictionary if you're not sure of certain pronunciations.

Speed or rate

Do you talk so fast that your audience can't keep up?

Do you talk so slowly that they are bored?

Do you pause briefly on occasion?

Do you vary between fast, slow, and paused speech?

Loudness or volume

Do you speak loudly enough so that everyone can hear you without straining to do so?

Do you speak softly enough so that you don't bombard the listener?

Do you vary the volume?

You may want to record a couple of sermons on audio- or video-cassette and evaluate the use of your voice. Is your voice pleasant to listen to? Do you use variety of rate and volume? I constantly have to remind myself to slow down, because my brain races in high gear, and preaching time is always short. I have to conscientiously vary the speed at which I speak. If you have problems in any of these areas, you may want to enroll in a public speaking course or work through a book on the subject. Get a confidant (perhaps your spouse) to point out how you can improve your sermon delivery. Above all else, speak with desperate passion. When your preaching has passion in it, delivery matters seem to take their appropriate places.

Afterword

Gutzon Borglum, a master sculptor, orchestrated the carving of one of the greatest pieces of large modern sculpture. The shrine to democracy portrays four faces of prominent U.S. presidents at Mount Rushmore National Memorial in the Black Hills of South Dakota. He had great pleasure in telling people that "the presidents' faces were always there; we just brought them in view."

Indeed, that is what expository preachers pursue—bringing the truth of particular scriptural texts into the view of the audience. You too can create sculpture from Scripture. Mix the dynamics of a vital spiritual life and the mechanics of sermon preparation, and you can go each time into the pulpit trusting the Lord of the Word to reinforce the Word of the Lord through you, his servant.

APPENDICES

These appendices relate to issues often brought up in Scripture Sculpture seminars, which have been conducted all over the world. They provide clarification, illustrations, elaborations, or technical comments on matters of biblical preaching that were dealt with in this book.

1 The Holy Spirit and Your Pulpit Effectiveness
2 The Benefits of the Original Languages for Preachers (Step 1)
3 Choosing a Text for Your Sermon (Step 2)
4 Introductory Notes on Grammar (Steps 1, 2)
5 The Perils of Principilization (Steps 1, 3, 4)
6 Hermeneutical Analysis and Homiletical Application of Narrative Texts (Steps 2, 4, 6)
7 Central Propositions: An Advanced Procedure (Steps 3, 4, 5)
8 Understanding Your Audience: Exegeting Culture (Steps 4, 6)
9 The Elements of a Competent Sermon Outline (Step 6)
10 A Sample Sermon Introduction (Step 6)
11 Forms of Sermon Introduction (Step 6)
12 Sermon Evaluation Questionnaire (Step 7)
13 Topical Exposition

Appendix 1

The Holy Spirit and Your Pulpit Effectiveness

By intention, the Scripture Sculpture sermon-preparation process is focused on the *mechanics* of expository preaching. Yet the best-prepared and best-preached sermon would turn into mere noise-making if the *dynamics* of the preaching process were not in place. The critical link between the mechanics and dynamics of the preaching process is the preacher's spiritual life. We ought to pursue an increasingly vital relationship with the Lord Jesus Christ by the Holy Spirit through faith in God's Word.

The following dynamics of preaching need to be in place around the preacher, the text, and the sermonic event. All of them relate to God, the Holy Spirit, the Third Person of the Trinity, in whose economy the preacher presently lives and ministers.

Personal Matters. Only spiritual, "prayed-up" preachers need enter the pulpit. A spiritual preacher abandons himself on the Holy Spirit, who in turn encroaches on the preacher's daily life. A spiritual preacher lives by the Holy Spirit. He not only asks and receives the filling of the Holy Spirit for the pulpit task but regularly beckons and yields to the Holy Spirit for control of his character.

Lewis Sperry Chafer said clearly and profoundly, "A Christian is a Christian because he is rightly related to Christ; but 'he that is spiritual' is spiritual because he is rightly related to the Spirit, in addition to his relation to Christ in salvation."[1]

Four New Testament commands in relation to the Holy Spirit apply to the Christian, but especially and first to the preacher.[2]

1. *Position yourself to be controlled by the Holy Spirit.* A command in the passive mood, Ephesians 5:18 balances the divine and human sides of the relationship. It is your responsibility to allow his ongoing control to take place. Much like a sailor positions the boat to catch the wind to move him on (cf. the Spirit and wind metaphor in John 3:6–8), we position our lives to be controlled by the Spirit. We invite and succumb to his control—daily, regularly, and intentionally.

2. *Cut out anything that would grieve the Holy Spirit* (Eph. 4:30). The full title of "the Holy Spirit of God" impregnates this command to not grieve the Holy Spirit. Obviously, the preacher looks for the manure and the muck of his life by inviting the Holy Spirit to run a fine-toothed comb, to shine a bright flashlight into the recesses of his being. Having identified personal messes, the preacher confesses his sin to move beyond receiving God's forgiveness to cleansing from all unrighteousness (1 John 1:9).

3. *Fan the flame of the Holy Spirit's enthusiasm for your spiritual vitality.* "Do not quench the Spirit," reads 1 Thessalonians 5:19, a corporate command with personal implications. He is more interested in your spiritual growth than you are. Pursue spiritual disciplines with a nonmeritorious motive. Those disciplines keep the spiritual flame burning. You become increasingly attached to the Trinity; detached from sin, Satan, and the world's values; and aligned to God's agenda and priorities before you engage in the discipline of preaching.

4. *Stay in tow as you keep in step with the Spirit.* To walk by the Spirit (Gal. 5:16), we, like an immobilized vehicle, are pulled

by a powerful tow truck. We can't hasten spiritual growth, for we have no power. But we can steer away or brake to slow down the process. Instead, we must let the Spirit pull us forward so that we do not fulfill the lusts of the flesh.

The preacher who is not living in vital relationship to the Lord Jesus by the power of the Holy Spirit adulterates his task. Instead, he should find the energy for the spiritual life in synergy with the Holy Spirit as he prepares to mount the pulpit for his sacred duty. Like the Holy Spirit, he too focuses on glorifying Jesus and clarifying truth (John 16:13–15).

Textual matters. The preacher not only relates appropriately to the Holy Spirit in his personal life, but also in his approach to the Scriptures. The combination of the Holy Spirit *and* the Word has been the traditional position, the evangelical mix, the orthodox balance in Christian history. Sermon mechanics primarily relates to the Word and sermon dynamics to the Holy Spirit, and we can't separate them. Each occasion of preaching that brings about godly results, in spite of the spiritual and skill deficiencies of the preacher, points to how closely the Word and the Spirit integrate and operate. The Spirit owns his Word for his sake and our sake even though we are sinful, stupid, or lazy.

The preacher counts on and seizes the Holy Spirit's relationship to the Bible because of the following dynamics:

1. *Inspiration.* Second Peter 1:21 attributes Scripture to "men moved by the Holy Spirit [who] spoke from God." Did you know that the Holy Spirit had you, your study, and your sermon in mind when he first inspired the text long ago? You can come to a text confident that the same Holy Spirit who inspired the text will see to it that you do the best you can within your limitations to glorify Jesus and clarify Scripture to your audiences. That dynamic provides godly confidence in the face of the most difficult of texts.

2. *Interpretation.* The Holy Spirit is your partner in the interpretive endeavor. That's why the spiritual vitality of the preacher is essential in studying, structuring, and arriving at the central proposition of the text. You clear out grievous and obvious sins, you express love to God and his Word, you prayerfully depend on the Holy Spirit

to understand a text "that we might know the things freely given to us by God . . . combining spiritual thoughts with spiritual words" (1 Cor. 2:12–13). Conscientious study of the Scripture combined with conscious dependence on the Holy Spirit better guarantees your approximation of the full truth of the Holy Spirit–inspired text.

3. *Illumination.* The Holy Spirit moves the preacher from approximation to clarity in understanding written revelation, and then to the conviction of "Thus says the Lord" or "The word of the Lord came. . . ." Illumination distinguishes between the non-Christian scholar who expertly interprets Scripture and the believing preacher who understands, accepts, submits, and applies its meaning. By the Holy Spirit who indwells him, the spiritual man understands the depths of God and appraises all things (1 Cor. 2:10, 15).

The Holy Spirit not only personalizes God's works in the believer (cf. the entire slate of his role in a believer's life), he energizes God's character in the preacher for personal dynamism—victory, power, fruit, Christ-likeness. Most important, the preacher internalizes God's Word by the Holy Spirit. He alone animates black print on a white page into a forceful weapon (Heb. 4:12); he clarifies the Word's applicational claim to the preacher and helps him appropriate it for personal understanding and obedience.

Sermon Matters. The total sermon event is surrounded by the Holy Spirit—before, during, and after the sermon.

Presermon. Your sanctified desire for the ministry, especially the preaching ministry, arises from the Holy Spirit's transformation of your heart. It is he who has authorized you to preach. That understanding of divine authorization and appointment consumes you during the sermon-preparation process. He gives you excitement during the discovery and the later delivery of your sermon. He assures you that he will compensate for your weakness and inadequacy, for your competency is from God alone (2 Cor. 3:5). He leads you into choices of biblical books and texts that would be most appropriate for your congregation.

Further, the Holy Spirit has preceded your coming to the audience. He is already convicting the world of sin, righteousness, and judgment (John 16:8–11). You are simply a part of that continuous interaction of God with people. You are not abandoned to your ingenuity at any time in the preaching process.

During the sermon. What is the unction, the anointing, that fills the language of preaching in terms of the preaching event? How does one get the anointing and feel the unction?

You can almost always tell what the "sacred anointing"[3] is not. It is not preaching in the flesh in order to entertain, manipulate, or control the audience. Now God uses your fleshly preaching for his purposes, since truth may leak out in the middle of your impressive presentation. The "anointing" of the preacher [I understand the "anointing" in 1 John 2:27 to be the Holy Spirit himself] is literally the "Spirited" preacher. Psyching yourself up for the contest like a wrestler gets ready for his opponent may be "spirited" but not "Spirited."

When you are "Spirited" in and on the pulpit, you sense divine ownership of your ministry, the sermon event, your very life. You read the Master's pleasure at your less-than-profitable service. You confidently submit to his orchestration of the people's response, since you are not in charge of the results. You intuitively know that you are being carried by his power throughout the presentation. He gives you the confidence and the demeanor that creates a powerful contagion between preacher and audience. The preacher remembers what he has prepared by the Spirit but yields to the Spirit's movements in spontaneously going beyond his preparation for what the Spirit additionally wants to say to the church. If you have ever experienced a listener affirm a part of the message that you didn't know you emphasized or even mentioned, the Spirit was doing his work of piercing that listener at exactly his point of need. An increasing awareness, surprise, and humility about the Holy Spirit's stewardship of the sermon comprises aspects of the anointing. You are not on that pulpit alone, left to your devices, gifts, or talents. You sense that he is there with you effecting his purposes in your audience.

Also while preaching, the Holy Spirit is the one who fosters the reality of God and his truth in your audience. It is he who will awaken the dead, sensitize their consciences, illuminate their minds, deepen their experiences, soften their hearts, and quicken their spirits and souls.

Even the faith that your less-than-perfect sermon is making a difference in people's lives in bringing them to salvation or maturity comes from divine unction. You will be filled with a spiritual sensitivity to the audience. He will give you discernment and boldness in calling for conversion, for change, for repentance, for response from them.

Postsermon. Though your sermon is done, the Holy Spirit is not done with your people. Just as the Lord Jesus promised his disciples—even those who didn't pen the Scriptures—that the Spirit of truth would guide them into all truth (John 16:11–12a), he will bring to remembrance his Word preached through you to his disciples today. He pursues them to their places of living, work, and play. He extends your application to new ideas and arenas of their obedience. He empowers their will to obey. He opens up opportunities to meet their inclinations since he has inclined their hearts toward opportunities during your sermon. And that means he has preceded your sermon again!

So nurture biblical spirituality and cultivate biblical preaching to become a mighty instrument in the hand of God, the Holy Spirit. Cover your sermon study, delivery, and results with prayer. Through prayer and study the ordinary human being becomes an extraordinary preacher by the power of the Holy Spirit who surrounds the preaching event with himself. To paraphrase 2 Peter 1:21, let it be said that these were "men moved by the Holy Spirit [who] spoke from God's word."

Appendix 2

The Benefits of the Original Languages for Preachers

A question that has often been asked in preachers' seminars is "Should one study the original biblical languages to preach well?" "What advantages are there in studying Greek and Hebrew for preaching?"

My answer is borrowed from Harold Hoehner, an esteemed colleague. The difference between studying in your own language and knowing the original languages is something like the difference between the picture on a black and white TV and on a color TV. The picture in color is more vivid and realistic. The more familiar you are with original languages, the better defined the text will be for you. Indeed, there are some precision decisions that cannot be determined with translations.

On the other hand, the black and white TV receives a signal and shows a good picture. You can follow the story very well as you watch it. A color TV is a wonderful luxury, the preferred product. If you can afford one, you'll probably decide it is worth the money. In the same way, get all the advanced training you can, but do not stop preaching just because you have not studied the biblical languages.

Many of God's greatest preachers have not been to seminary. Do not let your lack intimidate you. Dr. Lewis Sperry Chafer, the founder of Dallas Seminary and writer of a multivolume theology, did not know the original biblical languages. Further, the English language is versatile enough to give you an adequate meaning of the Bible. As you consult translations, dictionaries, and commentaries, you will be protected from error to a large extent. For instance, I recommend consulting a Bible that contains several versions to alert you to different translations of one passage. A good one is Curtis Vaughn, *The New Testament from 26 Translations* (Grand Rapids: Zondervan, 1967). Also, reading the Scripture in your mother tongue (if it is other than English) will give you beautiful angles on a given passage, especially as foreign translators worked from the original languages through their mother tongues into your vernacular!

If you do the work that I am recommending in this system of sermon preparation, you will not have to worry about not having enough material to preach. With some training in Greek and Hebrew, most of my advanced preaching students are more apt to face the problem of what to leave out of a sermon rather than finding enough to include.

When you can use the original languages in your study, your message will have greater precision, which will give you more confidence in your preaching. It is like using a detailed map to find your way around a city. A map with less detail might get you to where you want to go, but with the detailed map, you will be sure of the route each step of the way.

Appendix 3

Choosing a Text for Your Sermon

In the introduction to this book, I gave some of the advantages of preaching consecutive texts. On occasion you will need to depart from such a progressive or sequential preaching of a book. On Easter Sunday some years ago, I heard a message on Samson from the Book of Judges. The reason the pastor gave for preaching on Samson was that he had preached the previous chapter on the previous Sunday! Not only did he not meet the expectations of his audience, he did not seize the moment, since so many "Easter Sunday churchgoers" were there. They went home affirmed in their decision to attend church irregularly.

Here are some ways to choose the sermon text.

- *The biblical book.* This is the usual expository method. You preach each succeeding paragraph or passage. You must choose the biblical book by taking audience needs into account. If you were beginning a ministry among persecuted Christians in a hostile setting, you might choose to preach from the Book of 1 Peter.

- *The Christian calendar.* Take into account the great days of the church. Be sure to remember the Passion season (Palm Sunday, Good Friday, and Easter) and the Christmas season especially. Sometimes a group will observe other special days, such as a World Hunger Sunday or World Evangelization Sunday. The extent to which you relate to a special denominational or church calendar depends on your church's history, ties, and priorities.
- *The national calendar.* The United States has a Sunday set aside for Mother's Day. India celebrates Children's Day. Most countries highlight an Independence Day. Preaching appropriate messages for these special days is a good idea. Don't feel, however, that you have to recognize every holiday from the pulpit or preach a related message.
- *Special events.* Special events in the life of the church, such as the dedication of a church building, should feature a sermon related to the event.
- *Unusual events.* If the city or nation has gone through a national disaster, be sure to address it. I recall the Sunday after Prime Minister Indira Gandhi had been assassinated by her bodyguards. Hellish hatred had broken loose in New Delhi. Fear had descended on everyone. The nation was in mourning. A few brave souls made it to the services on that Sunday. They desperately needed a word from God, and it wasn't found in the next passage of the book I was preaching.

As you select the text, always keep your congregation in mind. What are their needs? What does God want them to hear this week, month, year? Even if you have to include these different calendars and events in a preaching schedule, you can still preach Scripture texts. In step 4 we deal with preaching more than one sermon out of a single text. If you do run out of such texts, you may want to think about topical preaching for special events.

APPENDIX 4

INTRODUCTORY NOTES ON GRAMMAR

In step 2 you had to use some tools of grammar to identify, evaluate, prioritize, and structure a passage. I enclose the following material on English grammar (especially for foreign students of English) to introduce or reintroduce you to the elements of English grammar. The material has been adapted from Frank X. Braun, *English Grammar for Language Students,* an excellent short introduction to the subject that can be easily understood and used for studying the English Bible.

Adjective: An adjective is a word used to modify (describe, limit, or qualify) the meaning of a noun or pronoun.

The child carried a *huge* balloon.

Adverb: An adverb is a word used to modify (describe, limit, or qualify) the meaning of a verb, an adjective, or another adverb.

He walks *swiftly.* They seemed *extremely* anxious. He walks *very* swiftly.

According to their meaning, most adverbs fit into one of the following groups. Examples are given for each group.

1. Time: *then, now, frequently*
2. Place: *here, there, somewhere*
3. Manner: *swiftly, gently, badly*
4. Degree: *very, extremely*

Articles: The *definite article (the)* points out one or more definite or particular things of a class.

> *The* boys in *the* front seats.

The *indefinite article (a* or *an)* denotes any one of a class of objects.

> *a* room
> *an* elephant

Clause: A clause consists of a subject and a predicate. It may constitute all or only part of a complete sentence. The following sentence consists of two clauses.

> *subject predicate*
> He received his pay when the work was done.

The *principal clause* (or main or independent clause) is a clause that can stand alone and make sense by itself.

> *He received his pay* is the principal or independent clause.

The *subordinate* or *dependent clause* is a clause that depends on the main clause for its meaning and cannot stand alone.

> *When the work was done* is a subordinate or dependent clause.

The subordinate clause is usually introduced by a subordinating conjunction (*although, because, if, that,* etc.), by an adverb (*where, whenever, when,* etc.), or by a relative pronoun (*who, whose, what, whom, that, which,* etc.).

Conjunction: A conjunction is a word used to connect words, phrases, or clauses. There are two kinds of conjunctions. *Coordinating conjunctions (and, but, or, nor)* connect words, phrases, or clauses of equal rank.

> The father *and* son are handsome.
> He may be poor *but* he is still proud.

Subordinating conjunctions (although, because, if, since, that, etc.) introduce clauses that are subordinate to the rest of the sentence.

> He stayed home *because* he had no money.

Direct Object: The person or thing directly affected by the action of the verb.

> The player passes *the ball.*
> John hit *his brother.*

Indirect Object: The indirect object is the person or thing indirectly affected by the action of the verb.

> He passed the sugar to *his guest.*
> He passed *his guest* the sugar.

The sugar is the object that is being passed (the direct object); *his guest* is the receiver of the direct object and is the indirect object.

Noun: A noun is the name of a person, place, or thing.

Pronoun: A pronoun is a word used in place of a noun to avoid awkward repetitions. Compare the following sentences:

> Tom thought Tom had lost Tom's money.
> Tom thought *he* had lost *his* money.

Gender: Gender is a change in the form or use of a noun or pronoun to denote sex.

> Masculine: *man, host, he, his*
> Feminine: *woman, hostess, she, her*
> Neuter: *book, it, its*

Verb: A verb is a word that expresses action or a state of being or condition. Verbs agree in person and number with the subject, and the form changes depending on the tense. English has both regular and irregular verbs.

> John *went* to school.
> The children *are watching* television.
> Visitors *will arrive* soon.

Tenses: The tense of a verb indicates the time of action. There are six tenses in English:

> *Present:* I talk. I am talking.
> *Past:* I talked. I was talking.
> *Future:* I shall talk. I shall be talking.
> *Present Perfect:* I have talked.
> *Past Perfect:* I had talked.
> *Future Perfect:* I shall have talked.

Mood: The mood of a verb indicates the intention of the speaker or writer. English has three moods. The *indicative mood* is used to state a fact or ask a question.

> They live in the country.
> Is he going?

The *subjunctive mood* expresses urgency, possibility, speculation, formality, and condition contrary to fact.

> Urgency: I demanded that she *see* me immediately.
> Formality: I move that the meeting *be* adjourned.

Contrary to fact: If I *were* you, I would go.

The *imperative mood* is used to express a command or a request. In English it is used only in the second person singular or plural. Other languages have a more complete imperative.

> *Pass* the sugar, please!
> Boys, *come* here!
> *Lead* us not into temptation!

Number: The number refers to the property of a noun, pronoun, or verb that indicates whether the reference is to one *(singular)* or to more than one *(plural)*. Subjects and verbs must agree in number. A pronoun must agree in number with the noun it replaces.

Preposition: A preposition is a function word used with a noun or pronoun to show its relation to some other word or words in the sentence. English has approximately sixty prepositions, such as *at, by, for, in, into,* etc. A prepositional phrase consists of a preposition and its object.

> He walked *into the store.*
> They sat *on the bench* and waited.

One preposition may have two or more objects.

> They traveled over *hill* and *dale.*

APPENDIX 5

THE PERILS OF PRINCIPILIZATION

Principilization is the theory of preaching that takes a passage, extracts a universal principle, and applies it to the contemporary context. For example, I heard a sermon on the topic "Our God is an abundant God," extracted from Genesis 1. Textual support came from the multiple things God created—many stars, many animals, many fish, many birds, and so on. The theological principle is true. Whether this text supports it needs to be thought through.

Principilization is a popular means of re-presenting the "truth" of a passage. The purpose of this appendix is to alert preachers to some of the dangers in this abstract endeavor. I am not saying that theological truth should not be extracted from the details of a passage, but I am saying that we should not use passages as mere illustrations of supposedly universal truths that exist apart from them.[1] The preaching method that has been proposed in this manual prevents the wrong kind of "principilization" that is advocated by some homileticians. In this method, I attempt to provide for biblical authority and contextual relevance—the reason for principilization as a homiletical strategy. (See appendix 6 on homiletical application of narrative, biographical, and historical texts.)

Here I articulate some difficulties with "principilization as a homiletical device." Several of these difficulties are pointed out by S. Greidanus in his highly technical work *Sola Scriptura.*[2] These principilizing tactics become especially acute while preaching narrative, biographical, and historically descriptive texts.

Principilization reduces redemptive history to the plane of moral history. The historical event in the development of redemption or the increments of special revelation become as insignificant as any noteworthy character or event in secular history. We could preach from Gandhi, Martin Luther King, church history, Plato, or cultural parables in this moral sense.

Ernest Best writes, "It is possible to obtain exactly the same results by allegorizing passages outside Scripture."[3] He uses the illustration of the fox and the crow in Aesop's fables. The piece of meat is the Word of God, the fox is the devil, and the crow is the Christian. The universal principle derived from this fable would be: "When the Christian thinks too highly of himself, he loses God's Word." That principle is highly preachable and theologically right.

Instead, Greidanus warns that "once one has taken a historical text as preaching text, he must take that text in accord with its own nature and no longer as illustration."[4] A narrative text is a fact of history and should be treated as such, not as a parable. "Whoever thinks it possible that God let a certain history be recorded in order to give 'teaching in pictorial form,' loses sight of the difference between a parable and piece of history."[5]

Principilization overlooks the importance and uniqueness of a particular narrative and happening—its factual character. If a historical text serves to "illustrate and depict concretely a certain 'truth,' then the factual character of such an event is not overly important since that illustration can equally well be given in a parable or allegory."[6] Historicity becomes secondary to the theological abstraction that is taught in the text. This view reduces the nature of Scripture to an exemplary case study textbook.

Instead, we maintain that theological truth is given a particular angle or twist in a given historical incident. Without the historical incident, the theological truth imbedded in it will not be there or even be true.

Principilization results in monotony because the uniqueness of each and every text is not caught. Interpreted atomistically, Holwerda says, "One can preach the same sermon on, e.g., Matthew 11:1–6 (the doubt of John the Baptist) and John 20:24–29 (the doubt of Thomas): Jesus Delivers from Doubt."[7] This monotony is usually overcome by the preacher's creativity. I often hear a man who follows a "principilization" method of preaching. He is highly imaginative and creative and an outstanding communicator, but the same principles are found in many texts. His preaching assumes archetypal principles that each text illustrates or manifests.

Instead, I suggest that this "least common denominator" view of theological truth give way to the particular theological truth of each text in redemptive history. The preacher's task is demanding and crucial in arriving at this central proposition and in contemporizing it to his audience.

Principilization limits preaching to the theological abilities and experiential categories of the preacher. The preacher can see less or more theological truth according to his theological training or human experience. While theological and experiential training deepens a preacher's insight into the Scriptures, his first task is to find what the Scripture says.

Principilization enters the exegetical study hoping to find some analogies between the early audience and recent audience. In a sense, we focus on our audience from the beginning of the preparation process. That focus, however, is not the first concern of the preacher if he desires to present an authoritative word from God. The principilization method cannot possibly do justice to the uniqueness of the text, because it first seeks some analogy between the people in the text and people today.

Principilization basically deals with how to spiritually adjust to this life. I find this kind of sermon everywhere. Some call this relevant preaching. I don't discount the fact that these preachers may be very relevant, but whether their preaching has biblical warrant is the question we are addressing here.

Sermons need to be faithful to the text as well as relevant. One does not and should not find relevance *outside* the central proposition of the text. I heard a sermon from Galatians 3:6–14 that had the following force: "God the Father is faithful, therefore, men should be faithful fathers." In this scheme, the Christian becomes the most important factor in the preaching process. Instead, the meaning of the text should be the first concern.

Principilization short-circuits the interpretation process by overlooking the discontinuity between the people then and the people today. A simple equation mark is placed between the past and the present so that then equals now.[8] Best calls this "direct transference" and soundly criticizes this method.[9]

Principilization puts the preacher in control of what he chooses to exemplify for the audience. There is no recognition of the historical gap between the early and present audiences. For example, should we require that conversions today be identical to Saul's? Should we call for the poor to give everything to the Lord (as in Luke 21)? Perhaps, the "universal principle" is that God breaks stubborn hearts (as in Paul's conversion), but there are many stubborn hearts that he does not break.

Unfortunately, in principilization the preacher chooses the particulars in which the passage relates to his audience. And many of the details of the passage become of little or no use in the sermon. Principilization emphasizes the preacher (and the hearer) over the text. Principilization makes the Scripture a passive object containing information of times gone by, possessing all kinds of truths that I, the preacher, the active knower, must distill from it and that I, the preacher, must *make* applicable.[10]

Principilization provides for psychological exegesis even without textual warrant. There is no doubt that principilization makes the text more interesting and therefore relevant. But the issue is whether such psychologizing does justice to the text. The question is whether Scripture itself presents to us a psychological description of the people included in its historical writing. If this is not the case, then neither I (nor principilization) may picture them psychologically.

Principilization spiritualizes the text. Jacob's physical struggle becomes our spiritual struggle; the physical blindness of Matthew

9 becomes our spiritual blindness. The homiletical remarks may be theologically right, but the question is if such spiritualization has anything to do with the text. Indeed, this is the allegorical method of interpreting and preaching. The historical text is treated as a concrete illustration of some moral truth found elsewhere, and if it is found elsewhere, why not preach that passage instead of this passage? Ask yourself, does this text have its own message?

Principilization reduces the faith to behavioral morality. In this way, the text is said to be relevant. The assumption that every text contains exhortations for proper behavior forces the text a priori into a moral mold that may or may not suit the text. The text is approached with this question (among others): What conduct is advocated here? But suppose it is not the intent of the text to answer that question? Historical texts are particularly stubborn on this point, but if the question is put to them anyway, the answer must somehow be deduced from the conduct of the person in the text.[11]

Appendix 6

Hermeneutical Analysis and Homiletical Application of Narrative Texts

Narratives, whether biographical, historical, or concerning miracles, make up a large portion of Scripture. One has to use interpretive discernment and sanctified imagination in preaching them. Perhaps the fundamental maxim in preaching narratives comes from Grosheide: "See the text first as part of the whole, and secondly . . . take the text in and by itself."[1]

Hermeneutical Analysis of Narrative Texts

In preaching narratives, the following kinds of exegetical analyses are needed.

Syntactical analysis. Analyze the grammatical and syntactical cues for movements within the narrative.

Movement analysis. Any change of subject, location, people, and so on indicates movement that needs to be considered in analyzing the text.

Rhetorical analysis. Repetition, *inclusio* (when the same words are used at the beginning and end of a passage to mark it off as a unit), and chiasm should be studied.

Verbal/lexical analysis. Repetition of words is a cue to take notice of the message. See my example in step 6 from Matthew 18: Forgiveness as freedom. Alter writes, "Repetition is a familiar feature of the Bible, but it is in no way an automatic device. When does literal repetition occur, and what are the significant variations in repeated verbal formulas?"[2]

Comparative analysis. One part of the text provides oblique commentary on another by use of "narrative analogy."[3] For example, Jacob, who deceived, is deceived by his sons. Or David, who committed adultery and murder, is unable to reprimand his family who commit rape and murder. Biblical authors were sophisticated writers employing rich narrative techniques.

Design analysis. AUTHORIAL SELECTIVITY. Great weight should be given to the author/editor of the text. He was writing purposefully, intentionally, and was composing a montage. The biblical authors had their own Hebraic logic of selectivity. They wrote with great sophistication.

Tzvetan Todorov proposes that

modern scholars are able to declare so confidently that certain parts of the ancient text could not belong with others: the supposedly primitive narrative is subjected by scholars to tacit laws like the law of stylistic unity, of noncontradiction, of nondigressions, of nonrepetition and by these dim but purportedly universal lights is found to be composite, deficient, or incoherent. (If just these four laws were applied respectively to *Ulysses, The Sound and the Fury, Tristram Shandy,* and *Jealousy,* each of those novels would have to be relegated to the dustbin of shoddily "redacted" literary scraps). Attention to the ancient narrative's consciousness of its own operations, Todorov proposes, will reveal how irrelevant these complacently assumed criteria generally are.[4]

The problem is that we impose our own laws and definitions of literary and stylistic unity—when and where an author should or should not digress or repeat his material!

AUTHORIAL INTENT OR PURPOSE. These define motives, relations, and unfolding themes. For example, Matthew intends the reader of his gospel to see Jesus as the King of Israel. Think through the impact of the crucifixion on the Roman who read the Book of Mark.

AUTHORIAL UNITY. Fragmentation is one of the great problems of narrative interpretation and preaching. We must pursue continuous interaction between the piece of the narrative in a particular text and the picture in the larger text. If there are gaps (such as logical, chronological, or psychological) in the narrative, they are part of the "artwork" of the writer/editor. We cannot impose modern literary standards on them.[5]

> *Theological analysis.* God's purposes in history are being enacted. Narratives "reveal the enactment of God's purposes in historical events."[6] What is the story of the book, the set of books to which it belongs, the testament, and the canon itself? Not everything can be preached today: Samuel hewing Agag to pieces, Samson committing suicide, Jeremiah preaching treason. These were right deeds required by God for that dispensation.
>
> *Anthropological analysis.* Human nature is "caught in the powerful interplay of the double dialectic between design and disorder, providence and freedom."[7] Witness, for example, the denials of Peter. The unique responses of individual characters to the events must be considered.

Here are four axes on which biblical narratives turn:

Historical/Circumstantial: a space/time event
Theological: the operations of God in the space/time event

Moral/Ethical: what should and should not be done in a given
   situation

Spiritual/Psychological: truth claims for appropriation and obedience by those who hear

Homiletical Application of Narrative Texts

See appendix 7 for an advanced procedure in sermon construction from nonepistolary texts.

- Apply the proposition that is derived from the text through
  hermeneutical analysis. Don't attempt to apply every detail in
  the text, for you will depart from hermeneutical faithfulness.
  The only way to guard against this is to come to a faithful central proposition of the text.
- Probe the four analytical axes for preaching resources: points
  to highlight, emphasize, illustrate.
- Create circumstantially/existentially analogous situations for
  application, not interpretation. For example, Barnabas being
  asked to see Paul after Paul had been converted could apply
  to your meeting with a formerly evil boss after hearing of his
  conversion.
- Do not try to make application of more than the major movements of the narrative. Again, you can explain and illustrate
  any detail of the passage, but all details of the text cannot be
  made into applications.

You may have heard of an interpretation and application of the
story of the Good Samaritan that is famous in church history: A man
went down from Jerusalem to Jericho. Jerusalem is the good city;
Jericho, the evil city. When you go down from one city to another,
the second city is always evil.

In the last section I gave you an example of a preacher who moved
from "God is a faithful Father who keeps his promises" (see Gal.
3:6–14) to "We must be faithful fathers who keep promises." This is

a topical exposition on the role of the father but not an exposition of a biblical text. Why? The CPT does not yield anything concerning human fatherhood.

In textual exposition, any biblically supportable truth is not necessarily a homiletically expoundable truth because it may not be a hermeneutically faithful truth.

Two Examples

Below I share two illustrations of preaching the same narrative—principipilization versus hermeneutical/homiletical precision. I am guilty of the former (since it lends itself to "preachability"), but I intend to pursue the latter.

Principipilization Preaching

Tips and Truths for Faith Fishing
Luke 5:1–11

I. The Ministry of Jesus: Jesus preaches to multitudes of people (vv. 1–3)
   A. Jesus was pressed by the multitudes on the lake (v. 1)
   B. Jesus preaches to the multitudes from a boat (vv. 2–3)
II. The Miracle of Jesus: Jesus performs the miracle catch of a multitude of fish (vv. 4–10a)
   A. Jesus commands Peter to cast his net (v. 4)
      Application: Faith-fishing tip #1: "Fish where fish are"
   B. Simon responds to Jesus' command (v. 5)
      Application: Faith-fishing tip #2: "Fish by faith not by sight"
   C. Jesus performs the miracle catch (v. 6)
      Application: Faith-fishing tip #3: "To fish is not to force"
   D. Simon calls for help to haul the fish (v. 7)
      Application: Faith-fishing tip #4: "Fish together whenever possible"
   E. The disciples are amazed and worship Christ (vv. 8–10a)
      Application: Faith-fishing tip #5: "Fishing must result in the worship of Christ"

III. The Mission of Jesus: Jesus puts Simon on a mission to catch men rather than fish (vv. 10b–11)
   A. Faith-following truth #1: Jesus proposes an alternate lifestyle ("from now on")
   B. Faith-following truth #2: Jesus promises a change of life ("I will")
   C. Faith-following truth #3: Jesus begins a lifetime process of fishing for men ("become")
   D. Faith-following truth #4: Jesus expects fishing for men to become a lifelong priority (v. 11)
   E. Faith-following truth #5: Jesus' mission purpose is lifesaving (the difference in fishing for fish and fishing for men)

Precision Preaching

Fishing People Fishing for People
Luke 5:1–11

I. The Ministry of Jesus: Jesus preaches to multitudes of people (vv. 1–3)
   A. Jesus is pressed by the multitudes by the lake (v. 1)
   B. Jesus preaches to the multitudes from a boat (vv. 2–3)
II. The Miracle of Jesus: Jesus performs the miracle catch of a multitude of fish (vv. 4–10a)
   A. Jesus commands Peter to cast his net (v. 4)
   B. Simon responds to Jesus' command (v. 5)
   C. Jesus performs the miracle catch (v. 6)
   D. Simon calls for help to haul the fish (v. 7)
   E. The disciples are amazed and worship Christ (vv. 8–10a)
III. The Mission of Jesus: Jesus puts Simon on a mission to catch men rather than fish (vv. 10b–11)
   A. A life-changing promise: Jesus promises a change of life ("I will make you")
   B. A lifestyle proposition: Jesus envisions a lifestyle of following him beginning immediately ("from now on")
   C. A lifetime process: Jesus develops a process of fishing for men throughout your life ("become")
   D. A lifelong priority: Jesus expects fishing for men to become a lifelong priority (v. 11—they left everything and followed him)

Now, why should I choose "precision preaching" over "principilization of the details" even though the former is as preachable (or even more so) than the other? For this passage, I have two reasons.

The first is because of the emphasis of the narrative. The climax feature of the narrative passage (known from hermeneutical analysis) is seen in verses 10b–11. We have to capture the climax in our sermon.

The second reason is that I had to think through what exactly the passage was describing and what it was prescribing. This distinction between prescription and description is critical. I cannot make principles or truths out of descriptions unless there is a sound exegetical case for them. If you are prone to make principles for your preaching, ask yourself about the exegetical grounding of those prescriptions. Otherwise, your sermon makes the Bible just the original, moralistic "instruction book" comparable to other wisdom literature of the ages.

The basic point is that each text has its peculiar proposition (or you can use the word *principle* if you mean it in the sense of proposition). The narrative passage is not simply an *illustration* but the actual *embodiment* of the theological truth. There is no pool of set, archetypal truths from which all passages draw their justification.

Appendix 7

Central Propositions

An Advanced Procedure

Here is a more advanced procedure to shape the central propositions of text and sermon for preaching. Our core method is a two-sided method linking the text side (steps 1–3) to the sermon side (steps 5–7) by the purpose bridge (step 4). A faithful and relevant sermon can be hewn by following the seven steps of the manual. However, you will find these extra processes useful especially when you have to preach from nonepistolary literature.

In this procedure, the central proposition of the text (step 3) and the central proposition of the sermon (step 5) are divided into two phases each. These subphases will better accomplish faithfulness, translatability, transferability, and application of the text.

I. The Central Proposition of the Text

A. *The Central Proposition of the Text (CPT)*. As you know, the central proposition of the text (step 3) derives from the structure of the text (step 2). We may also call the CPT the *exegetical* proposition, for the CPT is derived from exegesis.

In nonepistolary literature, an additional step needs to be introduced. Nonepistolary texts, such as biography, history, prophecy, or poetry show a marked literary phenomenon. They are highly "occasioned" writings, historically and theologically. While all biblical writing is "occasioned," nonepistolary Scripture maintains some historical and theological distance from us. Consequently, the exegetical proposition or the CPT will be even more controlled by the occasion the author addresses. The New Testament Epistles do distance themselves from us historically and culturally, but we inherit our theological identity by direct lineage from the early church. Since Old Testament and some Gospel biography, history, prophecy, and poetry writing relates to uniquely placed (pre-Pentecost) persons, events, and experiences, the text must be probed for its theological profit (not homiletical yet!) by interpretation and implication.

Here is the extra step. Before going to the purpose bridge (step 4), do an *expositional* proposition for the text side.

B. *The Expositional Proposition of the Text (EPT).* This proposition is a theological move, taking into account the long-range focus and profit of the text. This procedure is based on the premise that God was not talking only to the original audience but also to later audiences within and outside the biblical text (Rom. 15:4; 1 Cor. 10:11; 2 Tim. 3:16; 1 Peter 1:12).

The EPT must answer two critical questions.

The first key question is, *What is God saying in the central proposition of the text to subsequent believers that he was saying to the original audience?* To answer this question you consider the rhetorical strategy and purpose of the biblical author in providing a theological connection to later readers. A broad framework for this study depends on the constants of all time as imbedded in Scripture. Consider the four axes on which biblical narratives turn (see appendix 6, Hermeneutical Analysis and Homiletical Application of Narrative Texts, and the links mentioned on page 114) and look for the following motifs:

1. Motifs that reflect the nature of God, man, sin, evil, salvation, morality, Satan, the future, and so on. These are never changed in redemptive history.
2. Motifs that exhibit the created order, e.g., marriage. These are God's pristine preferences for all of history.
3. Motifs that transcend culture and time, e.g., homosexuality. These are not limited by geography, culture, or period.
4. Motifs that reflect individual or corporate spirituality, e.g., God's expectations in the Old Testament of the individual Israelite, of national Israel, of non-Israelite individuals and nations and in the New Testament of the individual Christian, of the local church, of the universal church, and of pagan nations.
5. Motifs that are repeated by words or events in Scripture, e.g., "God opposes the proud" (Prov. 16:16; James 4:6; 1 Peter 5:5) is found in Genesis 11:1–9, the Tower of Babel; in Isaiah 14:4–23, the oracle against the king of Babylon; and in Mark 14:27–72, Peter's denial.

Remember that some propositions cannot be applied to new audiences in the same way they applied to the first audience that heard them. This happens especially with Old Testament texts. Many passages are directly related to the theocracy of Israel, the Law, and the Old Testament covenants. For example, in Psalm 2:8, the anointed Son may ask for the nations as his inheritance. The EPT does not relate this verse to believers asking the Lord for the nations as their inheritance. Recall the first compatibility question from the purpose bridge (step 4)—*the author's purpose.* Otherwise, you will ambitiously place yourself in the place of the anointed Son and ask for property rights in every nation of the world without hermeneutical warrant! Instead, the EPT should be in keeping with how Christians should read Psalm 2:8: Jesus, as the anointed Son, is gifted with a worldwide inheritance. Note that this statement is processed through a New Testament theology of the anointed Son. You can take this expositional proposition of the text and pursue the purpose bridge.

The EPT must also answer another critical question: *In what sense is this proposition unique to this text in what it proposes?* If your expositional proposition is not unique in some way to this passage, it has compromised the content and the authority of this text. That is, "God opposes the proud" is not unique or specific enough for the passages that reflect it. Each of these texts gives a particular twist to that motif. For example, a unique kind of human pride and a particular kind of divine judgment are related in Genesis 11:1–9. Your EPT must not be a generic proposition abstracted, but a unique proposition specified. It is that particular, textual uniqueness that makes possible the next step of sermon preparation, the purpose bridge.

The reason for this extra exercise is to eventually facilitate a theological connection between the early audience and your audience. It also provides the resources for preaching without compromising the CPT. Here are some cautions in this process.

- Do not dehistoricize the text so that it is ambiguous.
- Do not deconstruct the text so that it is meaningless.
- Do not simply introduce a functional or dynamic equivalent of the parts of the CPT at this juncture of sermon preparation.
- Do not merely extract a moral principle from the CPT and work it into a generic proposition.
- Do not simply abstract a moral principle from the CPT for preaching (read about this danger in appendix 5).

The text is not just a case study or illustration of a timeless principle. It carries a proposition in itself that is unique in what it proposes.

Here is an example from Psalm 2 of moving from the CPT to the EPT.

CPT of Psalm 2

Theme: Since the King of heaven has installed his Davidic Son on the earth in Zion and declared his right to international rule,

Thrust: the rebellious kings of the earth must worshipfully submit to this ultimate King of the earth.

We know that the New Testament writers used Psalm 2 to point to Jesus as the ultimate King of the earth. So we can remove theocratic, Israel-related terms such as the *Davidic Son* and *Zion* and incorporate a theological interpretation from the New Testament. The rest of the EPT will reflect the CPT and remain intact, for this is how later believers understood the claims of Psalm 2.

EPT of Psalm 2

Theme: Since the King of heaven has installed and declared Jesus as the ultimate ruler of the nations,

Thrust: the kings of the earth must worshipfully submit to him.

Now your purpose bridge (step 4) can be drawn from this unique, text-particular, expositional proposition.

II. The Central Proposition of the Sermon

In this advanced procedure, the central proposition of the sermon (CPS), like the CPT, will have two phases.

A. *Expositional Proposition of the Sermon (EPS).* The mechanics here are the same as outlined earlier in this manual. Turn the purpose bridge into a question to provide the initial theme of the statement. Then contemporize the purpose facilitated by the EPT. Since the theme of the CPS is often initially in the form of a question, you would have to homileticize it for recall and impact. Pray, think, and work hard on the central proposition of the sermon.

B. *Central Proposition of the Sermon.* We can also refer to the CPS as the *homiletical* proposition. This is a highly stylized version of the EPS. It takes into account the preacher's rhetorical strategy and purpose, the design structure of the sermon, the mnemonic restatement of the homiletical proposition, and logical/emotional/ethical issues in the audience. At this stage of stylization, it will be driven by audience, communication, and application factors. Recognize, however, that if you stop short of this stylized and specific proposition, for lack of experience or time, you still will have a viable proposition to preach in the expositional proposition of the sermon.

Let me illustrate the entire process from a short, narrative passage.

1 Chronicles 12:32

And of the sons of Isaachar, men who understood the times, with knowledge of what Israel should do, their chiefs were two hundred; and all their kinsmen were at their command.

Central Proposition of the Text

CPT or Exegetical Proposition: I took into consideration the biblical and theological context of the divine appointment of David as the next king of Israel (v. 23) and came up with

Theme:	The characteristics of the two hundred leaders of the sons of Isaachar during the transition from Saul to David . . .
Thrust:	understood the times with knowledge of what Israel should do.

EPT: The expositional proposition of the text is facilitated by making theological connections from the exegetical proposition.

Theme:	The characteristics of spiritual leaders of God's people during times of divinely permitted change
Thrust:	must have understanding of the times with knowledge of God's revealed expectations of his people.

Notice the connections I have made: "sons of Isaachar" to "spiritual leaders," for spiritual leaders play the same role then and now; "Israel" to "God's people," for monarchical Israel does not exist now. The "transition from Saul to David" is connected to "divinely permitted change," for we know that all change is under God's control and permission. But monarchical change in Israel does not link to sociopolitical changes in the world, just to sociopolitical changes that God's people experience. There are other Old Testament passages on how Israel dealt with changes in the nations. "Understood the times" is changed to "understanding the times," for this is a call to God's leaders. "What Israel should do" is linked to "what God's revelation expects of his people," for the nature of revelation includes God's expectations. The sons of Isaachar knew what God wanted them to do from God's revelation.

Purpose Bridge

My audience is made up of future Christian leaders. Since we live in a period of massive change, my purpose bridge becomes: "to motivate future Christian leaders to understand the times and know what to do during the changes that their churches experience."

Central Proposition of the Sermon

I turn the purpose statement into a question for a preliminary and unpolished expositional proposition for my sermon.

EPS:

Theme: What does it take to become effective leaders during changing times in our churches?
Thrust: Sensitivity to culture (cf. understanding the times) and application of Scripture (knowing what God expects us to do).

I now sculpt a more stylized proposition.

CPS or Homiletical Proposition:

Theme: Effective spiritual leaders of congregations moving to the future.
Thrust: Exegete the world and execute the Word.

Advanced Procedure Chart

Text Side		*Sermon Side*

1. Study the Text
2. Structure the Text
3. Textual Proposition
   CPT or Exegetical
     Proposition
 	
Expositional
   Proposition of the
   Text (EPT)
	4. The Purpose
	Bridge
		5. Sermon Proposition
		   Expositional
		   Proposition of the Sermon
		    (EPS)
		
		   CPS or Homiletical Proposition
		
		6. Structure the sermon
		7. Preach the Sermon

If you find this addition of an expositional proposition tedious or ambiguous, don't do it. It is better that you pursue the method as it is laid out in the main section of this manual. There I have applied just the core method on nonepistolary texts such as Isaiah 19, Revelation 4, and Matthew 18. You would be more confident of faithfulness to the text in that way. As you gain more awareness of and experience in the core method, you may attempt what I suggest in this appendix.

APPENDIX 8

UNDERSTANDING YOUR AUDIENCE

Exegeting Culture

Biblical preaching without application leads to frustration in the audience even as application without authority leads to the eventual distrust of the preacher. But application that is not pertinent and oriented to the audience can lead to a dangerous notion. The audience leaves with the idea that the Bible does not relate to them or that it is good only for isolated instances in life.

As we know, the Bible has a comprehensive reach. Therefore, the preacher must promote the integration of biblical truth with life. The only way to integrate truth with life in preaching is by exegeting culture. Understanding one's audience is the second phase of sermon preparation (the first is to understand the Bible). The third is understanding one's self.

Exegeting culture is as much a discipline as exegeting Scripture. I like to duplicate step 1, Study the Text, in studying our audience. We must see life's details and interpret those details to give us the context for our preaching (and theologizing). I shall give you some guidelines as you develop this necessary ingredient of impacting preaching.

Seeing raw material in life's details. Great insight and material for illustration and application can be gained by observing your audience in the following arenas of their lives.

- The ways people communicate verbally and nonverbally
- How they live: their lifestyles, occupations, income, and spending
- Relationships: the roles of husbands, wives, children, extended family, and community
- The premises of their beliefs: their worldview, their values, their motivations

Finding resources for your preaching. You can find insightful resources to enhance your sermon by asking the following questions about your audience:

- What do they believe?
- What do they value?
- What do they need?
- What do they do? or How do they behave?

Find these resources in any expression of contemporary culture—newspapers, magazines, movies, the Internet, etc.

Connecting observations and interpretations about culture to your sermon.

1. To evoke needs in your introduction: Use the material that surfaced in your observations and interpretations to evoke needs pertinent to the purpose of your sermon that your central proposition will address. These "needs" may be spiritual, existential, philosophical, and even physiological. Utilize those findings in articulating an effective need in your introduction.

2. To illustrate your points: These studies will give you opening and closing illustrations and supportive material to use throughout the sermon.
3. To integrate truth and reality: At the point of cultural needs or tensions, find ways to integrate and apply the central proposition to their present life realities.

To make connections, observe the behavior of your audience and draw some conclusions as to its structure. For instance, if you observe that people carry many keys (for their house, car, office, etc.), ask yourself what is the deep structure of this surface behavior? What are people afraid of? What do they hope for? If they carry many keys, they may have a deep desire for security and ownership. If you are in a passage that refers to God's protection, such as Psalm 46, or God's ownership of all things, such as Psalm 24, you can illustrate and apply it from this aspect of your audience's life.

Understand how people would like to behave as opposed to how they actually live. This understanding will reveal an important resource and connection for preaching. For example, people may want to be generous but live selfishly. Being generous takes time and money, both of which people think they have little. If you are in the Good Samaritan passage, you can illustrate and apply it from this aspect of your audience's life.

You need to understand what your audience already believes without their needing proof or justification. In the West, people believe that one can actually control life (or aspects of it); in other parts of the world, people believe that one cannot actually control life (any aspect of it!).

If you were preaching a passage about God's rulership over lives, the truth would apply differently in the two contexts. In the West, you would challenge people to yield control of their lives to God. In other parts of the world, you would stress that people take responsibility for certain aspects of life even though God is sovereign over all.

A final comment: The best way to know your audience is to spend time with them. Spend time with them in their work and at home.

Be with them at the hospital and cemetery. Read what they read. Understand their questions. Get inside their minds and lives. As you integrate your exegesis of the Word with your exegesis of the world, your communication will be richer, deeper, more relevant, interesting, dynamic, and impacting.

APPENDIX 9

THE ELEMENTS OF A COMPETENT SERMON OUTLINE

The following elements of a competent outline, with slight alteration, are taken from Al Fasol's *Essentials for Biblical Preaching: An Introduction to Basic Sermon Preparation.*[1] It is more important that you are conscious of meeting these criteria in a topical sermon than in a textual sermon, because many of these will be met as you seek to elicit the outline from the text in textual exposition.

1. The outline should have a strong, clear relationship to the title.
2. Each major point should discuss only one aspect of the title or theme.
3. Each major point should be distinct from other points.
4. Each major point should be written as a complete sentence.
5. Each major point should be written in the present tense.
6. Each major point should have approximately equal value in the development of the sermon.

7. The points should be organized in whatever order and style (e.g., logical, poetic) will best communicate the textual interpretation to a particular congregation.
8. The outline should contain specific rather than general wording.
9. Each major point should have a textual basis.

Appendix 10

A Sample Sermon Introduction

In step 6 we divided the introduction into three parts: pre-introduction, introduction, and sub-introduction.

Pre-introduction. This segment has nothing to do with the sermon but has everything to do with the speaker and the audience. Often these are words of greeting and show some continuity with the earlier part of the service or the audience or the hosts.

Main introduction. Again the main introduction has four characteristics:

- Gets the attention of the audience
- Raises an appropriate need
- Orients the audience to the theme or the central proposition of the sermon
- States the purpose or destination of the sermon

Sub-introduction. The sub-introduction sets the "context of textual authority" for the sermon while reviewing a previous sermon or the title of the series or announcing the text.

I will illustrate these ingredients of a strong introduction from the "Get Off the Chair!" (Rev. 4) sermon mentioned in step 6. This sermon just happens to be the one I preached while writing step 6. Let me show you how I attempt to apply what I have suggested in step 6. What I would say is in italic.

TITLE: Get Off the Chair!
—Needs to tease the reader into taking a second look and thinking a second thought
—Accurate, clear, short, and interesting

TEXT: Revelation 4:1–11

MAIN INTRODUCTION. [Attention getter related to the theme. Notice this is not a good story for a good story's sake. Appropriate illustrations must be found.]

Four mothers who had priests for sons were declaring the esteem with which these men were addressed. The first said, "My son is a priest. When he walks into a room, the people call him 'Reverend Father.'" The second said, "My son is a monsignor. They address him, 'Your Excellency.'" The third said, "My son is a cardinal. The people call him, 'Your Lordship.'" The fourth mother was not sure of what to say: "My son is 6 feet, 10 inches, and 350 pounds. When he walks in, people get up and say, 'Oh, my God!'"

Orientation to the theme: "Creature Deification by Christians"

This morning I want to speak about creature deification—or more specifically, Christians (not Christ's) usurping claims to divinity. We have robbed God of his nature or attributes and focused them on ourselves. Other religious frameworks claim the nature of God as dwelling in humans. In our culture and in evangelicalism especially, we have usurped the omni-functions and feelings of deity. We concentrate glory, honor, and power on ourselves. We prefer to sit on the throne of our lives and think we live forever and ever: "Flirtations with divinity" or "self-deification." It is true that the ultimate religious question that man needs to face is whether he will worship someone transcendent or himself.

I call these "throne strategies" of men. Wider culture has wider throne strategies, for example, biotechnology and genetic engineering—the desire to play creator of life itself. However, Christians too have functionally occupied the throne of heaven in our own lives. We practically role-play God so that God cannot play his practical role. Like Eve of old, we are enchanted with deification, tempted by the possibility of acting divine, fascinated by self-sovereignty. Let me suggest three areas where we flirt with deification.

Raising a need: Christian Throne Strategies and Their Vanity

Throne Strategy 1: This is an "independence through proprietorship" syndrome—a flirtation with sovereignty, the assumption of independence and ownership of my life. I have independent ownership of my life. I am the owner, maker, source of my life. If I don't look after myself, nobody will.

How else can we explain, for instance, our quiet living in sin, our patterns of wrongful behavior, habits of sin that we pursue in our lives? Any time we sin we are assaulting God's throne. It is an act of cosmic treason; a coup d'état against God's government. In sinning, I make the rules. How else can sin be explained except if we are claiming sovereignty? In the old worldview, humankind was the measure of all things. Now the individual is the measure of all things.

I include an illustration of a Christian justifying his lifestyle of sinning, and then I go on to raise the need.

Yours may not be an overt sin and a covert lifestyle such as that, but every time I am tempted to sin, I am tempted to sovereignty. There is the assumption of independence. We declare that we are the ultimate arbiters of the laws. Sin and the Christian faith reconcile in me. If you are carrying sin in your life today—anything from anger to adultery, you are your own sovereign! It is an illusion of divinity. You are sitting on the throne of heaven in your life. Would you mind getting off the chair?

I go on to a couple more need raisers in this sermon and end each of those with "Would you mind getting off the chair, please?" I spend a substantial amount of time—15 to 20 percent of the time—raising the need, so that people will be yearning for some resolution or solution.

There is room for only one to be seated on the throne to receive worship. We need to get off the chair!

Here I review the subject again.

Independence, invincibility, importance "syndromes" are thoroughgoing characteristics of Christian deification. Only deity can claim these without exaggeration or error. We cannot, ladies and gentlemen. We cannot and should not.

Statement of purpose:

My purpose today is to challenge us to dethrone ourselves in view of the central throne of heaven. I want us to resist temptations to deification by cultivating the protocol of heaven when it comes to the sovereign chair—the Lord God Almighty, Holy, Eternal Creator who is the only one worthy of worship.
Let us look at how to get off the chair that we have wrongly occupied.

SUB-INTRODUCTION

I refer you this morning to the throne vision passage of Revelation 4. As you may know, as part of the continuing apokalypsis, the apostle John is invited into the throne room of heaven to receive spiritual ("I was in the Spirit") and prophetic (his vision is a composite of Isaiah's and Ezekiel's visions) foresight and insight. The question that Revelation addresses is: Who will be king—the exclusive sovereign God or an idolatrous substitute? Christ or Caesar in the past? Christ or Antichrist in the future? and by implication, Christ or anything else including yourself in the present?

As you also know, Revelation 4 follows Christ's messages to the churches of Asia (Rev. 2–3). Five of the seven churches experienced disloyalty to Christ as their number one spiritual problem. Soon there were to be options for deception that would deceive even the elect if possible.

Revelation 4 is pregnant with significance of how we relate to the chair of heaven and history. Let's get in with John's invitation. Peek into heaven—to observe, learn, and apply heaven's protocol on how to relate to the Sovereign who is worthy of your worship. Two of over a dozen heavenly hymns in Revelation are found here. Our focus is not on the song of the living creatures, which Bishop Heber immortalized for us in "Holy, Holy, Holy."

Here I sneak in the CPS in raw form and will do so at the end of the sermon as well.

Our focus is on the second song—the song of the elders. "Our sovereign God is worthy of our worship because he is the significance, superintendent, and sustainer of all people." He is the owner and operator of the universe; he is the maker and manager of all history— macro- and micro-history. Therefore, we can't sit in his chair. Would you mind getting off the chair, please?

Appendix 11

Forms of Sermon Introduction

Here is a partial list of types of material to use in an introduction secured from some Dallas Theological Seminary notes on introduction. I have classified them as pre-introduction and introduction possibilities.

Pre-Introduction

- Commendation
- Reference to previous speaker
- Acknowledgment of introduction
- Reference to a special season

Main Introduction

If you recall the four ingredients of an effective main introduction, you may want to write in the precise ingredient each entry on the following list attempts to meet.

- Startling statement
- Challenging question(s)
- Serious or pertinent incident
- Humorous or amusing incident
- Vivid word picture
- Concrete illustration or example
- Definition(s)
- Quotation(s)
- Paradoxical statement
- Statement of problem
- News item
- Witty items
- Object lesson
- Parable or proverb
- Reference to popular book or TV/radio program
- Current event

APPENDIX 12

SERMON EVALUATION QUESTIONNAIRE

While teaching homiletics at Dallas Theological Seminary, Haddon Robinson and fellow faculty devised a very useful questionnaire to evaluate one's preaching. It is still used in the preaching laboratories of Dallas Theological Seminary—one of the foremost homiletical training institutions in the world. I have adapted and expanded this questionnaire, which is found in Robinson's *Biblical Preaching*,[1] in keeping with the preaching method in this book. The following questions will guide you as you structure your sermons and evaluate your delivery. The principles represented are universally applicable since they are based on the way humans send and receive messages. Ask yourself these questions each time you write and preach a sermon.

Organization of the Sermon

Title

Is it contemporary? impacting? accurate? clear? short? Does the title explicitly or implicitly reveal what the sermon is about?

193

Pre-Introduction

Does it show awareness of what has gone before in the service?

Does it take into account the audience's attitude toward the speaker?

Does it show common ground with the audience?

Is there a discernible transition between the pre-introduction and the main introduction?

Reading of the Text

Is the passage properly declared?

Is time given to find the passage?

Is it read well? (Text may be declared and/or read in several places. See step 6.)

Main Introduction

Does it get attention?

Does it raise some need directly or indirectly?

Does it orient you to the theme? or to the main proposition? or to the first point?

Is the sermon purpose stated?

Is it the right length?

Sub-Introduction

Is the background of the text or sermon clear?

Does it contribute to the theme, purpose, or main proposition in a useful way?

Body Structure

Are the points clearly stated? sufficiently anchored? adequately validated? properly explained and applied?

Is the development clear? Is the overall structure clear?

Does the sermon have a central proposition? Can you state it?

Are transitions clear? Do they serve as review?

Is there a link between the points?

Do the main points relate back to the main proposition?

Are the subpoints clearly related to their main points?

Design Structure

Is the sermon arranged in an impacting way?

Does it evidence logical arrangement? chronological
  arrangement?

Does it show sensitivity to the psychological or sociological issues
  that may be raised by the sermon?

Conclusion

Does the sermon build to a climax?

Is there an adequate summary of ideas?

Is the central proposition of the sermon restated?

Are there effective closing appeals or suggestions?

Content

Central Proposition and Exegesis

Is your theme or topic significant?

Is it appropriate to the text and audience?

Is the central proposition of the text stated or evident in the
  sermon?

Is the sermon anchored in good exegesis?

Do you tell your audience where you are in the text?

Is the analysis of the theme full? sensible?

Are the arguments convincing?

Does the content show originality?

Supporting Material

Is the supporting material integrally related to its point?
Is it interesting? varied? specific? sufficient?
Do you state the points to be illustrated?
Do you make a transition from the points to the illustrations?
Are the points connected to the audience?
Are points restated or reviewed after their illustrations?

Application

Are applications made in the right places?
Are they customized to the audience? Are they concrete?
Do they answer the "so what" question?
Do they answer the "now what" question?

Style

Is all grammar correct?
Is vocabulary concrete? vivid? varied?
Are the words used correctly?
Does the choice of words add to the effectiveness of the sermon?

General Effectiveness

Audience Adaptation

Is the sermon adapted to the audience's interests? attitudes?
Is it related to their knowledge?
Does it meet needs?

Review of the Delivery

Intellectual Directness

Do you speak loudly enough?
Do you speak directly to the audience?
Are you friendly?
Does your delivery sound like lively conversation?
Do you stumble over the pronunciation of any words?

Oral Presentation

Do you use a pleasant tone of voice? Do you articulate clearly?
Do you vary the pitch, loudness, and rate?
Do you use pauses effectively?

Physical Presentation

Is your entire body involved in the delivery? Do you use gestures?
Are the gestures spontaneous? definite?
Do you try to avoid distracting mannerisms?
Do you use good facial expression?
Do you make appropriate and adequate eye contact?
Are you aware of the audience's response?

APPENDIX 13

TOPICAL EXPOSITION

We have noted the two ways of expounding Scripture—textually and topically. The Scripture Sculpture process delineates *textual* exposition. But theologians, preachers, and evangelists have often indulged in the *topical* exposition of the Scriptures as well.

The key difference between textual and topical exposition lies in the source and development of your central proposition. In a textual sermon, the theme and development of the sermon is controlled by the text. In a topical sermon, the preacher chooses the theme and governs the development of the sermon. For this reason alone, some professors of preaching call on us to fall on our knees to weep and wail in repentance after preaching a topical sermon!

I see the primary advantage of topical preaching not in its ease of preparation, for good topical preaching can demand time; nor in its higher potential for relevance, for you should depart from your textual servings to address immediate issues topically; but in the great advantage of inculcating a biblically informed worldview among biblically illiterate audiences who do not hold the Bible as authoritative in their lives.

I suggest the following method in pursuing topical sermons.

Topical Exposition

1. Choose your topic.
2. Limit your topic.
3. Build your topic.
4. Preach your topic.

1. *Choose your topic.* You will find hundreds of topics in reference Bibles such as Thompson's or Nave's or Dake's or in a concordance. These topics are usually Bible-driven and lend themselves more to instruction than motivation. For example, what does the Bible say about "heaven" or "grace" or "money"?

You may also choose topics that are audience-driven. That is, your choice of a topic, though the topic itself is addressed or anticipated in the Bible, is audience-driven. For example, if there has been a tragedy in your city, or should your people need a study on "giving," you would bring that particular topic to the Bible. Mix your preaching themes and topics between Bible-driven and audience-driven choices. The former addresses "knowledge and belief" needs while the latter focuses on "conduct and behavior" needs of the audience. Homiletical growth and development lie in picking topics that the Bible addresses and are also needed by the audience.

I chose as my topic for a pastor's conference "finishing the work that God has given you to do." Knowing that my audience faced such issues as moral failure, ministry apathy, spiritual distraction, and discouragement prompted me to choose a topic the Bible addresses by statement, author-intended example, and repetition in the Old and New Testaments. I would later "homileticize" or "stylize" the topic.

2. *Limit your topic.* Limiting your topic will make your preparation easier and your choices of texts less random. One of the questions homileticians ask of a typical, three-point, topical sermon would be why there are three rather than four or five or more texts and points. You should prevent that negative judgment on your seeming arbitrariness by narrowing, defining, and specifying your topic. You may have heard of the preacher who said, "To make up for my twenty-point sermon of last week, my sermon today will be pointless." Select one limited theme (the word *theme* applies to tex-

tual, thematic, and topical sermons) that you can probe in your study and preach well.

"Finishing the work God has given you to do" applies more specifically to pastoral leaders than simply "finishing well," a topic for a general audience. We could go to numerous texts and examples in Scripture to illustrate "finishing well" or "not finishing so well." Since you are limited by time and occasion, limit your topic to seize the preaching opportunity. Any desire to be exhaustive will exhaust you in preparation and your audience in your delivery.

3. *Build your topic.* Here you engage text and topic in interaction for developing the sermon. Use extreme care in building your topic. First, find pertinent Scriptures and then build subtopics, not the other way around. While you may derive topics from audience needs, build your subtopics according to the available Scriptures to explain or support your topic's development. Do not create your topical edifice and attempt to find Scriptures to buttress your choices. For, if you do, you will fall into the problem of "proof texting." It is at this point that topical preaching goes awry. We can support almost anything with scriptural proof texts! Proof texts become pretexts for whatever *we* want to say to our people, rather than receiving what *God* says on a particular matter and turning them into the structure of the sermon.

How does one avoid arbitrary choices of subtopics, the fragmentary mining of texts, and personal penchants in building subtopics?

a. Build on prescriptions, assertions, or statements. These are especially found in epistolary or in wisdom literature. You can confidently gain subtopics for your topic from straightforward declarations or imperatives in Scripture. If a text plainly or by implication teaches truth on a topic, you may freely choose it to develop your topic.[1] In many ways clear assertions ("God loves a cheerful giver," 2 Cor. 9:7) and prescriptions ("give in proportion to prosperity" [based on 1 Cor. 16:2]) are the easiest in topical development.

Real problems for topical preaching, however, arise in finding topics and subtopics in the narratives, in biographies, and especially in the practices of biblical characters. Textual authority will seem weak if we preach on "why we should travel in pairs," using Noah's pairing of his animals; or Jesus' commissioning disciples to minister in pairs; or the feature of apostolic pairs (Paul and Barnabas). It is very difficult to exegetically or theologically justify that "traveling in twos" was being proposed for present obedience. You may be able to focus the topic on "the advantages of traveling with at least one colleague in itinerant ministry" and make a pretty solid case. Yet such advantages—mutual encouragement, accountability, and mentoring—themselves have to be deduced from examples in narrative that may or may not have been within the author's purpose. Thus I propose a threefold grid in utilizing narratives for developing topical sermons.

b. Build on purpose, plot, or pattern of the text. To choose a valid point or subpoint from the narratives (this holds good for textual expositions as well), you need to detect and demonstrate your points from:

(1) The *purpose* of the text. If I am preaching on the topic of "God's protection of his covenant people," I may go to 2 Kings for one of my points. But I would need to lodge that point ("God's protection proves his exclusive presence among his people") in the *purpose* of 2 Kings. The first part of 2 Kings is written to underscore that "there is a God in Israel, and the man of God is in Israel, over and against God's absence in the powerful nations that captured them."

(2) The *plot* of the text. The author's "plot" is one way the author accomplishes his purpose and a critical way to discover that purpose. The purpose of the Gospel of John is clearly stated—"these have been written that you may believe that Jesus is the Christ, the Son of God; and that believing you may have life in His name" (20:31). John not only narrates the miracles of Jesus, but also the Lord's interaction with specific characters to accomplish his purpose. You can detect John's use of Nicodemus (or the Samaritan woman or Thomas) moving from questions to interest to belief to commitment to Jesus. If you would then preach the story of Nicodemus according to

these movements in the entire gospel, you can be clear and certain of textual authority.

(3) The *pattern* of the text. If the author's plot has to do with characters, the author's pattern emerges from words, phrases, and concepts. You can explore the themes of "belief," "light," and "eternal life"; "provision of physical food by Jesus points to spiritual provision" from the author's patterns. Let's say you want to preach about believing on Jesus the Shepherd. You can obviously go to Psalm 23 but also to the "Shepherd of Israel" (e.g., Isaiah 40; Ezekiel 34) motif of the OT, which reveals a pattern of God's leadership of Israel. Your final point can relate Jesus' claim to be the Good Shepherd (John 10) as one of his assertions to deity so people can believe on him.

Going back to the sermon on "the advantages of traveling in pairs in itinerant ministry," if you detect authorial purpose or plot or pattern to make a case from Luke and Acts for the topical imperative, then you possess textual authority. Otherwise, you will appear to be random in your choice, pursuing your personal interests while communicating mere opinion. Sadly, your people's opinions are as valid as yours and do not facilitate their obedience to God's truth. You can communicate your opinion as *preference* from observed textual phenomenon; just don't present it as a *prescription* for obedience. If an apostolic practice is supportable by prescription elsewhere or repeated for emphasis, you stand on surer textual ground. If not, your audience is left to your whimsical imagination and capricious ingenuity without adequate textual or theological foundations. The closer you can establish the connection between Scripture's propositions, the author's purpose, and your main points, the more authority your topical sermon will contain and convey. You can thus preserve the biblical integrity of your topical sermon.

From the author's repeated statements of Jesus setting his face toward the cross and Paul fulfilling his life intentionally, I chose my specific topic "Finishing the work God has given you to do." I also limited my choices of subtopics to clear texts. I found two rather clear texts that turned into a two-point structure for a topical sermon.

a. John 17:4. Jesus glorified the Father by accomplishing the work he was given to do.

b. Acts 20:24. Paul did not count his life as dear to himself in order that he may finish his course (cf. his final declaration in 2 Tim. 4:7).

4. *Preach your topic.* Your topical sermon will evidence the same features as a textual sermon. Come up with a stylized central proposition, a clear structure, and then preach that sermon.

The central proposition of the topical sermon, as does any proposition, consists of theme and thrust. My theme on this topic is simple: "Finishing the work God has given you to do?" (stylized later to "Going the distance in God's work despite failures, fatigue, and fear"). My thrust carries a multiple edge (another prominent feature of topical sermons is that they carry multiple thrusts):

a. Seek to glorify God in all you do and you will finish the work God gives you to do (John 17:4) (stylized later to "Increase God's weight in all aspects of your God-given ministry to go the distance in God's work").

b. Don't consider your life as dear to yourself and you will finish the work God gives you to do (Acts 20:24) (homileticized later to, "Decrease your self-importance in all aspects of your God-given ministry to go the distance in God's work").

I must admit that topical sermons elicit and unleash creative energies in choosing a focused, specific, pertinent, and interesting topic, and then in structuring and preaching it. I encourage you to balance textual and topical exposition in all your preaching. Textual sermons resemble vitamins that fortify, while topical sermons are more like aspirins that pacify. Your people need both strengthening and soothing. As long as you are disciplined and honest enough to exegetically and/or theologically justify your textual choices and interpretations as within the range of the authors' (divine and human) meaning, you should be safe and confident. You would still have to kneel often, but you wouldn't have to repent for having preached a topical sermon.

Notes

Preface

1. A quick survey of what we can learn from great preachers in history is found in G. Ray Jordan, *You Can Preach: Building and Delivering the Sermon* (New York: Fleming H. Revell, 1951), chap. 5, from Clement of Rome (bishop, ca. 88–ca. 93) to Phillips Brooks (1835–1893).

2. This phrase itself is a plagiarism! Webb Garrison (*The Preacher and His Audience* [Westwood, N.J.: Fleming H. Revell, 1954], 256), points out Charles L. Moore's ("the Highest Type of Originality in Literature," *Current Literature* 50 [1911]: 100) criticism of Faust, who is supposed to have borrowed the first half of the entire piece. In reading most of the homiletical works of the last century, I found unstated borrowing was a regular feature! I shall attempt to state where I got ideas singularly or en masse.

3. I do not include this anecdote to disparage preachers in the great city of Bombay (now Mumbai). My friends did find a fine church there. I guess I should have preached more on the problems of alcoholic consumption.

4. A comprehensive homiletical textbook would consider everything from the person of the preacher to his presence in the pulpit, from his personal holiness to the use of his voice. This manual focuses only on the *mechanics* of preaching, occasionally dabbling in the full range of subjects of a homiletics textbook. Several basic textbooks, such as those by Broadus and Robinson, are cited in the bibliography.

Introduction

1. Here are some excellent definitions of expository preaching. Braga and Hayden focus on the content of the sermon. Robinson and the Committee on Biblical Exposition include methods and goals of expository preaching.

An expository sermon is "one in which a more or less extended portion of Scripture is interpreted in relation to one theme or subject. The bulk of the material for the sermon is drawn directly from the passage and the outline consists of a series of progressive ideas centered around that one main idea" (James Braga, *How to Prepare Bible Messages* [Portland, Ore.: Multnomah, 1969, 1981], 53).

An expository sermon is one that "begins with a substantial passage of Scripture and allows the principal thoughts of that passage to become the outline for development and the basis for application" (Edwin V. Hayden, "What Is Expository Preaching?" in Charles R.

Gresham, ed., *Preach the Word: Guidelines to Expository Preaching* [Joplin, Mo.: College Press, 1983], 1–2).

Expository preaching is the communication of a biblical concept, derived from and transmitted through a historical, grammatical, and literary study of a passage in its context, which the Holy Spirit first applies to the personality of the preacher, then through him to hearers (Haddon Robinson, *Biblical Preaching* [Grand Rapids: Baker, 1980], 20).

Bible exposition is communicating the meaning of a text of Scripture in terms of contemporary culture, with the specific goal of helping people to understand and obey the truth of God (Committee on Biblical Exposition, 1982).

Step 1: Study the Text

1. Step 1 is related to what is commonly known as Bible study methods. Starter books on the subject include:

Fee, Gordon D., and Douglas Stuart. *How to Read the Bible for All It's Worth*. Grand Rapids: Zondervan, 1982.

Finzel, Hans. *Observe, Interpret, Apply: How to Study the Bible Inductively*. Wheaton: Victor, 1994.

Hendricks, Howard G., and William D. Hendricks. *Living by the Book*. Chicago: Moody Press, 1991.

Traina, Robert A. *Methodical Bible Study: A New Approach to Hermeneutics*. Grand Rapids: Zondervan, 1985.

Wald, Oletta. *The Joy of Discovery in Bible Study*. Minneapolis: Augsburg, 1975.

2. Robert Traina, *Methodical Bible Study: A New Approach to Hermeneutics* (Grand Rapids: Zondervan, 1985), 181.

3. Roy B. Zuck, "Biblical Hermeneutics and Exposition," in *Walvoord: A Tribute*, Donald K. Campbell, ed. (Chicago: Moody Press, 1982), 19.

4. Eugene Lowry, *How to Preach a Parable: Designs for Narrative Sermons* (Nashville: Abingdon, 1989), 36–37.

5. Harold W. Hoehner, "Ephesians," in *The Bible Knowledge Commentary: New Testament* (Wheaton: Victor, 1983), 639.

Step 3: The Central Proposition of the Text

1. I prefer *proposition* as the clearest term. Philosophically, proposition is more consistent with an evangelical bibliology; and homiletically, the term is consistent with homiletical tradition. For example, John Broadus, in *On the Preparation and Delivery of Sermons*, 4th ed., rev. Vernon L. Stanfield (San Francisco: Harper and Row, 1979), written in the late 1800s, used *proposition* (see chap. 8).

A more recent text also refers to *proposition*. After identifying coordinates and subordinates (cf. our step 2), the authors write: "The next step in text analysis is the formulation of a propositional statement, a statement which distills and crystallizes the central thought of the text. The propositional statement is a statement out of which the sermon theme eventually evolves" (Joel Gerlach and Richard Balge, *Preach the Gospel: A Textbook for Homiletics* [Milwaukee: Northwestern, 1978], 25).

Seven years after I put down the sermon regimen in writing, I found this fine text by Gerlach and Balge, which reflects some of the sequence that I am proposing in this manual. This again confirms the suspicion that I declared in my introduction—even contemporaries have been stealing my supposedly original thoughts! I also gratefully acknowledge the homiletics program at Dallas Theological Seminary over my student and professorial years. Haddon Robinson, Duane Litfin, John Reed, and colleagues too numerous to name have influenced me in concept, practice, and explanation.

2. Quoted in John R. W. Stott, *I Believe in Preaching* (London: Hodder and Stoughton, 1982), 226.

3. Haddon Robinson, *Biblical Preaching* (Grand Rapids: Baker, 1980), 33. Homiletics students exposed to *Biblical Preaching* will detect my plagiaristic indebtedness to Haddon Robinson in my step 3.

Step 4: The Purpose Bridge

1. If there is anything that claims a semblance of originality in this manual, it is the mechanics of the process I explain in step 4, or the movement from step 3 to step 5 through step 4. Even advanced students seem to be helped in their grasp of the homiletical process each time this process is taught.

2. John Killinger writes: "Sermons often flounder because their preachers have not identified their purpose before beginning them. . . . The ingredients of a good sermon may be present—a spiritual attitude, clever ideas, good language, illuminative analogies or illustrations—so that both the preacher and the congregation are puzzled about why nothing seems to *happen* in the sermon. But without a clear purpose in mind the preacher cannot hope to accomplish much" (*Fundamentals of Preaching* [Philadelphia: Fortress, 1985], 48).

3. Jay Adams has entitled his book *Preaching with Purpose* (Grand Rapids: Baker, 1982), pointing us to the *telos* or the goal of the sermon. He makes a powerful case for justifying the purpose of everything in a sermon—from illustration to outline structure. See especially his chapter 1: "The Centrality of Purpose."

4. Gerlach and Balge call purpose "the telic note: What does the Holy Spirit intend to accomplish through this Word of God in the hearts and the lives of his people on this occasion?" (*Preach the Gospel*, 26). "Purpose is the central issue. The preacher's purpose in preaching, the purpose of the text, the purpose of the sermon content, of the organization, of the style, of the illustrative materials, of the type of delivery used—all of these and much more are crucial to good preaching" (3).

As mentioned earlier, the approach of Gerlach and Balge is akin to what I have proposed in steps 1–4, except that they want the telic note to influence the propositional statement. The purpose of the sermon should not influence the propositional statement of the *text*. It will certainly affect the propositional statement of the *sermon*.

5. "A sermon is a revelation of some aspect of the reality of God in reference to some human need or condition" (Theodore P. Ferris, *Go Tell the People* [New York: Scribners, 1951], 17).

6. For some who may be interested, I must address a point that Eugene Lowry (*How to Preach a Parable: Designs for Narrative Sermons* [Nashville: Abingdon, 1989], 37) brings up. He castigates the propositional form of preaching because of its deductive orientation in most preachers. "Those who suggest a thematic statement in the sermon preparation process often place it exactly between biblical work and sermon formation. The unintended result is to divide the work, with the whole process unwittingly imagined as an hourglass on its side: biblical work narrowing toward the thematic sentence, which then opens into sermon formation."

Here is my response. First, in this method the thematic statement is not in the middle of the process. The purpose bridge is the link between biblical work and sermon formation. Second, "a deductive orientation" arises from the system of education that seminarians go through rather than something that is intrinsic to the sermon process being presented here. It is inductive as it arrives at the thematic sentence. Whether the sermon will be deductively or inductively oriented depends on step 4—the design/structure of the sermon. Third, I appreciate the "artsy" side of Lowry's suggestion.

Instead like "experienced novelists and other narrative artists who never quite know where the story will go or should go," preachers must stay open. "We, too, need to maximize our capacity to keep open throughout the preparation process. The theme sentence seems not to encourage that openness" (37).

I suggest that an effective "purpose" bridge preserves and provides for the preacher to be an artist while not allowing an uncontrolled and uncontrollable "openness" that will rob the text of its authority.

Step 5: The Central Proposition of the Sermon

1. John R. W. Stott, *I Believe in Preaching* (London: Hodder and Stoughton, 1982), 225.

2. John A. Broadus, *On the Preparation and Delivery of a Sermon*, 4th ed., rev. Vernon L. Stanfield (San Francisco: Harper and Row, 1979), 38.

3. John Killinger, *Fundamentals of Preaching* (Philadelphia: Fortress, 1985), 44. Killinger suggests that the sermon idea comes from the lectionary text for the Sunday or out of the blue "at any time." For expository preaching, this "idea" comes from the text and is processed through the "purpose" of the sermon.

Or as Gerlach and Balge put it: "The propositional statement attempts to express the central thought or the main thrust of the text in terms of its telic note. It accents what the inspired writer accents. It subordinates what he subordinates. It is not a sermon theme, though on occasion it may be. The sermon theme is embryonic within the propositional statement and emerges from it" (Joel Gerlach and Richard Balge, *Preach the Gospel: A Textbook for Homiletics* [Milwaukee: Northwestern, 1978], 27).

By the way, if you want to preach a subordinate point of the text as the main point of your sermon, you have to shorten the text that you are considering as the preaching portion for the occasion.

4. J. H. Jowett, *The Preacher, His Life and Work* (London: Hodder and Stoughton, 1912), 133.

5. Some refer to the "theme" as "subject" (for example, Haddon Robinson). In my experience, students tend to confuse the homiletical subject (or theme) with the grammatical subject of a sentence, which is most often a prominent noun. Consequently, I have given up the term *subject* for the less confusing term *theme*. The theme also works well for topical subjects or themes that one may pursue. Whether textual or topical, the sermon has one theme.

Henry Grady Davis, *Design for Preaching* (Philadelphia: Fortress, 1958), writes against erroneous kinds of subjects or themes (chap. 5). He calls them "Indefinite Subjects," "Fuzzy Subjects," and "Noun Subjects." He defines a subject or theme thus:

> What's in a subject?
> > At least: What is to be talked about.
> > Always: The limits within which to keep.
> > Or more: A hint of what is to be said.
> > At most: All that the sermon will say. (58)

6. Contemporization is not "face-value" relevance. Ernest Best calls such a theory of interpretation "direct transference" and shows several legitimate faults with the "face-value" theory of interpretation (*From Text to Sermon: Responsible Use of the New Testament in Preaching* [Edinburgh: T. and T. Clark, 1978], 57ff.). Very simply, situations are

never the same between the early world and ours; concepts change their meanings between original and contemporary usage; there may be no equivalent concept today. Best gives the example of the concepts of *sheep* and *shepherd* as lacking in Eskimo culture. (His last two problems with this theory come from a subevangelical view of the Scriptures and are not dealt with here.) An outstanding short work, it is much clearer on what we are not supposed to do in preaching than on what we are to do.

For those interested in the technical aspects of hermeneutics and homiletics, I make the following assertion: We cannot always hold to the "face-value" theory of relevance. In the didactic literature of the Epistles, this relevance is easier to pursue than in the nonepistolary literature. I hold to "face-value meaning" arising from a historical-grammatical theory of hermeneutics. I also hold to a dynamic-equivalence theory of homiletics consistently built on the historical-grammatical hermeneutic. We cannot equate or confuse the hermeneutic strategy with the homiletic strategy.

Step 6: Structure the Sermon

1. Sermonic unity is demonstrated and preserved in this sermon-making process in the following ways:
   • Unity is found through the central proposition of the text (step 3).
   • Unity is found in the purpose of the sermon (step 4).
   • Unity is found in the central proposition of the sermon (step 5).
   • Unity is found in the structure of the sermon (step 6).
   • Unity is found through review, repetition, and restatement of the CPS or the main points or the subpoints as the sermon moves forward to a conclusion (steps 6 and 7).

2. Over a century ago, Henry Ward Beecher (*Yale Lectures on Preaching*, First, Second, and Third series, [New York: Ford, Howard & Hulbert, 1887]) spoke about the need for variety:

> No man ever preaches, all the time thinking of producing specific effects, without very soon being made conscious that men are so different from each other that no preaching will be continuously effective which is not endlessly various; and that not for the sake of arresting attention, but because all men do not take in moral teaching by the same sides of their minds. (Series 1 53)

Beecher classified hearers in the following way:

Intellectual: For these the more logical and more mathematical the better.
Emotional: These are "fed by their hearts."
Aesthete: These look for beauty of style and charm of imagination in the sermon to accept its truth.
Mystic: "These do not receive anything unless it is hazy!"

He then goes on to speak to his young students on "How to Meet Differing Minds." A couple of quotes on variety will suffice.

> The hotel proprietor does not serve what he likes best. He spreads his tables for the benefit of the community at large. (Ibid., 55)

> If a man can be saved by pure intellectual preaching, let him have it. If others require a predominance of emotion, provide that for them. If by others the truth

is taken more easily through the imagination, give it to them in forms attractive to the imagination. If there are still others who demand it in the form of facts and rules, see that they have it in that form. Take men as it has pleased God to make them; and let your preaching, so far as concerns the selection of material, and the mode and method by which you are presenting the truth, follow the wants of the persons themselves, and not simply the measure of your own minds. (58–59)

You are not practised workmen until you understand human nature, and know how to touch it with the Divine truth. (61)

3. These characteristics are found in Broadus, *On the Preparation and Delivery of Sermons*, 4th ed., rev. Vernon L. Stanfield (San Francisco: Harper and Row, 1979), 81ff.

4. Or, application deals with two basic connections:
"As Then—So Now" (Positive)
"As Then—So Not Now" (Negative)
Adapted from R. C. H. Lenski, *The Sermon: Its Homiletical Construction* (Grand Rapids: Baker, 1968), 228.

5. Biblical counselors have always included the "Now what?" in their ministries. Jay Adams in *Preaching with Purpose* (Grand Rapids: Baker, 1982), makes an effective point:

Clearly, the Sermon on the Mount possesses an abundance of deliberate *how to*. Why have homileticians failed to notice a very obvious fact? Possibly because, unlike biblical counselors, they have not been aware of the importance of implementation in change. If you want your preaching to be effective, then, like Christ, be sure to give *how-to* help. (129)

Typically, Bible believing preachers have implemented neither positively nor negatively, by *how* or how *not* to. They have been good at telling congregations what to do, but notoriously poor at telling them how to do it. (138)

6. Beecher, *Yale Lectures*, Series 1, 171. Evans echoed the opinion a long time ago as well: "The preacher needs to have wide-open eyes. To have eyes and see not, ears and hear not, is fatal to the preacher" (William Evans, *How to Prepare Sermons and Gospel Addresses* [Chicago: Colportage, 1913], 61).

7. The definition of an illustration includes its connection with the audience. Beecher calls illustrations "covert analogies." "The groundwork of all illustration is the familiarity of your audience with the thing on which the illustration stands. . . . substantially, the mode in which we learn a new thing is by its being likened to something which we already know" (*Yale Lectures*, Series 1, 155).

8. Haddon Robinson (*Biblical Preaching* [Grand Rapids: Baker, 1980], 79–96) has three helpful "developmental questions" to which the central proposition and individual points must be submitted. 1. "What does it mean?" 2. "Is it true?" and 3. "So what?" The other use of these three questions is to pinpoint places where illustrations are needed.

9. This section on conclusions is summarized from the author's entry in the *Leadership Handbooks of Practical Theology, vol. 1: Word and Worship*, gen. ed. James D. Berkley (Grand Rapids: Baker, 1992), under "Conclusions," 94–95.

10. Milton Crum Jr., *Manual on Preaching: A New Process of Sermon Development* (Wilton, Conn.: Morehouse-Barlow, 1988, 88), sees the need for synopsis in the follow-

ing two sequences. "A Synopsis summarizes the verbal content of the sermon in two or three segments, in their order of presentation, usually either as

1. Situation-Complication
2. Resolution
or
1. Situation
2. Complication
3. Resolution

In either case, the conclusion will relate to resolution.

Step 7: Preach the Sermon

1. A sermon that is written out is qualitatively different from the extemporaneous sermon. "By this [an extemporaneous sermon] it is meant preaching without writing. It is not to be mistaken for preaching without adequate preparation." J. J. A. Proudfoot, *Systematic Homiletics* (New York: Fleming H. Revell, 1903), 300. Adequate preparation includes the discipline of writing out the sermon.

2. A few that we recommend at Dallas Seminary are Sue Nichols, *Words on Target* (Richmond: John Knox, 1963); A. Duane Litfin, *Public Speaking: A Handbook for Christians,* 2d ed. (Grand Rapids: Baker, 1992); Reg Grant and John Reed, *Telling Stories to Touch the Heart* (Wheaton: Victor, 1991).

3. According to A. W. Blackwood, the "three tests of literary style in a sermon" are clearness, interest, and beauty (*Expository Preaching for Today* [Nashville: Abingdon, 1953], 49). In my opinion, interest and beauty are the twin edges of razor sharp style in effective communication.

4. You could hide your half sheets in your Bible just in case you forget some sermon points. But you will soon find this covert operation unnecessary if you put steps 1–7 into practice. Again, in no case should you be dependent on your notes. Would you want an outstanding soloist to sing from her score or a movie actor to check his notes in the middle of the movie? An integral part of the preaching ethos is lost when you are dependent on notes.

5. When you are preaching your sermon, you should ask yourself, "How would I feel about me if I were sitting where they are, listening to me?" Technically, this question relates to the attitude of the audience toward the speaker. They are sizing up your competence, modeling, friendliness, trustworthiness, enthusiasm, and presence, which are all dimensions of your credibility. Your delivery will influence their attitude toward you in several of these areas.

6. Check Spurgeon on articulation: "Do give a word a fair chance; do not break its back in your vehemence, or run it off its legs in your haste." *Spurgeon's Lectures to His Students,* condensed and abridged by D. O. Fuller (Grand Rapids: Zondervan, 1955), 93.

Appendix 1: The Holy Spirit and Your Pulpit Effectiveness

1. Lewis Sperry Chafer, *He That Is Spiritual,* rev. ed. (Grand Rapids: Zondervan, 1967), 23.

2. In this outline of the "Holy Spirit and the Christian," I dispel any doubts that I engage in "topical exposition." I attempt to restrict unlimited trails by textual limits—only four commands relate the Holy Spirit to the Christian; and a practical limit—the time allotted to the sermon. One time the pastor of a church leaned over to whisper just before I

took the pulpit, "Preach for as long as the Holy Spirit leads you in the fifteen remaining minutes of our service!" A practical consideration indeed.

3. Phrase borrowed from the title of Tony Sargent's *The Sacred Anointing: The Preaching of Dr. Martyn Lloyd-Jones* (Wheaton: Crossway Books, 1984). "Lloyd-Jones refers to it ["unction" or "the sacred anointing"] as a 'divine afflatus' which drives the preacher to the point where he has so surrendered himself to the dynamic of God's power that he is driven along as he proclaims the message" (31).

Appendix 5: The Perils of Principilization

1. For a well-articulated and careful approach to the principilization process, see Timothy S. Warren, "A Paradigm for Preaching," *Bibliotheca Sacra* 48 (October–December 1991): 463–860. See also J. Daniel Hays, "Applying the Old Testament Law Today," *Bibliotheca Sacra* 158 (January–March 2001): 21–35.

2. S. Greidanus, *Sola Scriptura: Problems and Principles in Preaching Historical Texts* (Toronto: Wedge Publishing Foundation, 1970).

3. Ernest Best, *From Text to Sermon: Responsible Use of the New Testament in Preaching* (T & T Clark, 1978).

4. Greidanus, *Sola Scriptura*, 58, citing B. Holwerda

5. Greidanus, *Sola Scriptura*, 61.

6. Ibid., 61.

7. Ibid., 64.

8. Best, *From Text to Sermon*, 70.

9. Ibid., 57ff.

10. Greidanus, *Sola Scriptura*, 93.

11. Ibid., 80.

Appendix 6: Hermeneutical Analysis and Homiletical Application of Narrative Texts

1. S. Greidanus, *Sola Scriptura: Problems and Principles in Preaching Historical Texts* (Toronto: Wedge Publishing Foundation, 1970), 60; see also Robert Alter, *The Art of Biblical Narrative* (New York: Basic Books, 1981), whose comments are included in several points in this appendix.

2. Alter, *Art of Biblical Narrative*, 21.

3. Ibid.

4. Ibid., quoting T. Todorov, *The Poetics of Prose*, trans. Richard Howard (Ithaca, N.Y.: Cornell University Press, 1977), 53–65.

5. Ibid., 18.

6. Ibid., 33.

7. Ibid.

Appendix 9: The Elements of a Competent Sermon Outline

1. A. Fasol, *Essentials for Biblical Preaching: An Introduction to Basic Sermon Preparation* (Grand Rapids: Baker, 1989), 65–66.

Appendix 12: Sermon Evaluation Questionnaire

1. Haddon Robinson, *Biblical Preaching* (Grand Rapids: Baker, 1980), 217–20.

Appendix 13: Topical Exposition

1. For those interested in hermeneutics, I propose three levels of unpacking a text's meaning. *Statement, implication,* and *extrapolation* comprise the range of meaning in a text. *Statement* repeats and reports what the text says. *Implication* arises from what the *human* author intended to say in the text and provides for continuities between the original audience and us. *Extrapolation* is embedded in the human author's statement and implication and is explored through biblical and systematic theology, as intended by the *divine* author for discontinuities between the original audience and us. For example, while the contemporary issue of abortion is addressed by biblical statement and implication, cloning issues need to be addressed by extrapolation. You may consult the first ("Selected Issues in Theoretical Hermeneutics") and second part ("Levels of Biblical Meaning") of my series "Methodological Proposals for Scriptural Relevance," *Bibliotheca Sacra* 143 (January–March 1986; April–June 1986): 14–25; 123–33.

BIBLIOGRAPHY

Adams, Jay E. *Preaching with Purpose.* Grand Rapids: Baker, 1982.

Alter, Robert. *The Art of Biblical Narrative.* New York: Basic Books, 1981.

Baird, John E. *Preparing for Platform and Pulpit.* Nashville: Abingdon, 1968.

Baumann, J. Daniel. *An Introduction to Contemporary Preaching.* Grand Rapids: Baker, 1972.

Beecher, Henry Ward. *Yale Lectures on Preaching,* First, Second, and Third Series. New York: Ford, Howard & Hulbert, 1887. 3 vol. in 1.

Berkley, James D., gen. ed. *Leadership Handbooks of Practical Theology,* vol. 1: *Word and Worship.* Grand Rapids: Baker, 1992.

Best, Ernest. *From Text to Sermon: Responsible Use of the New Testament in Preaching.* Edinburgh: T & T Clark, 1978.

Blackwood, A. W. *Expository Preaching for Today.* Nashville: Abingdon, 1953.

———. *The Fine Art of Preaching.* New York: Macmillan, 1943.

Braga, James. *How to Prepare Bible Messages.* Portland, Ore.: Multnomah, 1969, 1981.

Braun, Frank X. *English Grammar for Language Students: Basic Grammatical Terminology Defined and Alphabetically Arranged.* Ann Arbor, Mich.: Edwards Brothers, 1947.

Broadus, John A. *On the Preparation and Delivery of Sermons.* 4th ed., revised by Vernon L. Stanfield. San Francisco: Harper and Row, 1979.

Crum, Milton, Jr. *Manual on Preaching: A New Process of Sermon Development.* Wilton, Conn.: Morehouse-Barlow, 1988.

Davis, Henry G. *Design for Preaching.* Philadelphia: Fortress, 1958.

Demaray, Donald E. *Introduction to Homiletics.* Grand Rapids: Baker, 1990.

Evans, William. *How to Prepare Sermons and Gospel Addresses.* Chicago: Colportage, 1913.

Fasol, Al. *Essentials for Biblical Preaching: An Introduction to Basic Sermon Preparation.* Grand Rapids: Baker, 1989.

Fee, Gordon D., and Douglas Stuart. *How to Read the Bible for All It's Worth.* Grand Rapids: Zondervan, 1982.

Ferris, Theodore P. *Go Tell the People*. New York: Scribners, 1951.

Finzel, Hans. *Observe, Interpret, Apply: How to Study the Bible Inductively.* Wheaton: Victor, 1994.

Gerlach, Joel, and Richard Balge. *Preach the Gospel: A Textbook for Homiletics.* Milwaukee: Northwestern, 1978.

Grant, Reg, and John Reed. *Telling Stories to Touch the Heart*. Wheaton: Victor, 1991.

Greidanus, S. *Sola Scriptura: Problems and Principles in Preaching Historical Texts.* Toronto: Wedge Publishing Foundation, 1970.

Hayden, Edwin V. "What Is Expository Preaching?" in Charles R. Gresham, ed., *Preach the Word: Guidelines to Expository Preaching,* Joplin, Mo.: College Press, 1983.

Hendricks, Howard G., and William D. Hendricks. *Living by the Book*. Chicago: Moody Press, 1991.

Hoehner, Harold W. "Ephesians," in *The Bible Knowledge Commentary: New Testament.* Wheaton: Victor, 1983.

Holwerda, B. "De Heilshistorie in de Prediking," *"... Begonnen Hebbende van Mozes ... ,"* 79–118. Terneuzen: Littooij, 1953. (First published in *GTT*, 43 [1942], 349–70, 381–403.)

———. *Dictaten Historia Revelationis.* Veteris Testamenti. Kampen: Comité voor de uitgave van de college-dictaten van wijlen Prof. B. Holwerda, 1954, 1961.

Jordan, G. Ray. *You Can Preach: Building and Delivering the Sermon.* New York: Revell, 1951.

Jowett, J. H. *The Preacher, His Life and Work.* London: Hodder and Stoughton, 1912.

Killinger, John. *Fundamentals of Preaching*. Philadelphia: Fortress, 1985.

Koller, Charles W. *Expository Preaching without Notes*. Grand Rapids: Baker, 1962.

Lenski, R. C. H. *The Sermon: Its Homiletical Construction*. Grand Rapids: Baker, 1968.

Litfin, A. Duane. *Public Speaking*. Grand Rapids: Baker, 1981.

Lowry, Eugene. *How to Preach a Parable: Designs for Narrative Sermons.* Nashville: Abingdon, 1989.

Nichols, Sue. *Words on Target*. Richmond: John Knox, 1963.

Perry, Lloyd M. *A Manual for Biblical Preaching*. Grand Rapids: Baker, 1965.

Proudfoot, J. J. A. *Systematic Homiletics*. New York: Revell, 1903.

Reu, M. *Homiletics*. Minneapolis: Augsburg, 1924, 1950.

Robinson, Haddon. *Biblical Preaching*. Grand Rapids: Baker, 1980.

Spurgeon, Charles. *Spurgeon's Lectures to His Students.* Condensed and abridged by D. O. Fuller. Grand Rapids: Zondervan, 1955.

Stott, John. *I Believe in Preaching*. London: Hodder and Stoughton, 1982.

Todorov, Tzvetan. *The Poetics of Prose.* Translated by Richard Howard. Ithaca, N.Y.: Cornell University Press, 1977.

Traina, Robert. *Methodical Bible Study: A New Approach to Hermeneutics*. Grand Rapids: Zondervan, 1985.

Vaughn, Curtis. *The New Testament from 26 Translations*. Grand Rapids: Zondervan, 1967.

Wald, Oletta. *The Joy of Discovery in Bible Study*. Minneapolis: Augsburg, 1975.

Warren, Timothy S. "A Paradigm for Preaching," *Bibliotheca Sacra* 48 (October–December 1991): 463–86.

Whitesell, Faris D., and Lloyd M. Perry. *Variety in Your Preaching.* Westwood, N.J.: Revell, 1954.

Wilkinson, Bruce and Kenneth Boa. *Talk thru the Bible.* Nashville: Thomas Nelson, 1983.

Willmington, H. L. *Willmington's Bible Handbook.* Wheaton: Tyndale, 1997.

Zuck, Roy B. "Biblical Hermeneutics and Exposition," in *Walvoord: A Tribute,* edited by Donald K. Campbell. Chicago: Moody Press, 1982.

Scripture Index

Genesis

1   160
11:1–9   174, 175

1 Chronicles

12:23   177
12:32   177

2 Chronicles

7:14   39

Ezra

7:10   54, 55, 59, 61

Job

1–2   42
3–14   42
15–21   42
19:25   43
22–31   42
32–37   42
38–41   42
41   42

Psalms

2   175, 176
2:8   174
23   40, 202
24   182
46   182
51   106
117   35, 74, 75

117:1   74
117:2   74
119   106
133   125
133:1   107
133:2–3   107

Proverbs

16:16   174

Isaiah

14:4–23   174
19   179
19:18–25   80
40   202

Ezekiel

34   202

Daniel

9:24   45
9:24–27   45
10:2   45
10:3   45

Jonah

1:1–2   40
1:3–14   40
1:15–2:10   40
3:1–10   40
4:1–11   40

Matthew

9   163–164
11:1–6   162
14:26   37
16:18   38
18   179
18:21   119
18:21–22   119
18:21–27   119
18:21–35   117
18:28–35   119
22:36–37   24
28:19   37, 38

Mark

14:27–72   174

Luke

5:1   169, 170
5:1–3   169, 170
5:1–11   169, 170
5:2–3   169, 170
5:4   169, 170
5:4–10   169, 170
5:5   169, 170
5:6   169, 170
5:7   169, 170
5:8–10   169, 170
5:10–11   170, 171
5:11   170
17:11–14   40
17:11–19   40
17:15–19   40
19:29–30   22
19:29–40   22

19:30   22
19:31–32   22
19:33   22
19:34   22
19:35–40   22
21   163

John

3:6–8   146
10   40, 202
10:30   38
16:8–11   148
16:11–12   150
16:13–15   147
17:4   203
20:24–29   162
20:31   201

Acts

1:1–8:3   39
1:8   39
8:4–12:25   39
13:1–28:31   39
20:24   203

Romans

12   69
15:4   173

1 Corinthians

2:10   148
2:12–13   148
2:15   148
7   106

10:11 173
12 69
16:2 200

2 Corinthians

3:5 148
9:7 200

Galatians

3:6–14 163, 168
5:16 146
6:10 106

Ephesians

2:1–3 39
2:4 39
4 105
4–6 50
4:1–6 107
4:7–10 69, 100
4:7–11 68, 88, 89, 100
4:7–13 69
4:7–16 68, 69, 80, 82, 88, 89, 90, 99
4:11 73, 100
4:11–13 71, 73
4:11–16 69, 87, 88

4:12 39, 69, 73, 100
4:12–13 69, 88, 89, 100
4:13 38, 73, 100
4:14 69, 100
4:14–16 69, 88, 89, 100
4:15 100
4:15–16 100
4:16 100
4:30 146
5:18 146
6:1–3 75
6:1–4 75
6:4 76
6:10 50, 61, 62, 63, 64, 101
6:10–11 101
6:10–12 49, 56, 61, 63, 68, 70, 76, 80, 82, 93, 101, 104, 105
6:11 62, 63, 64, 101
6:11–12 62, 63, 64, 101
6:12 49, 62, 63, 64, 101
6:13–17 83
7:11 68
7:12 68

Colossians

1:1–2 45
2:12 45
3:1 38
3:2 45

1 Thessalonians

4:13–18 39
4:18 39
5:19 146

2 Timothy

3:16 173
3:16–17 25
4:7 203

Hebrews

4:12 148

James

4:6 174

1 Peter

1:12 173
2:13 43

3:7 44
4:7 69
5:4 39
5:5 174

2 Peter

1:21 147, 150

1 John

1:9 146
2:27 149
4:4 39
4:19 38

Revelation

2–3 106, 190
4 107, 179, 187, 189, 190
4:1–11 91, 114, 187

ABOUT THE AUTHOR

God has permitted Dr. Ramesh Richard to become a global spokesman for the Lord Jesus Christ. Dr. Richard is a professor at Dallas Theological Seminary, where he teaches across three academic departments. He is also the founder and president of Ramesh Richard Evangelism and Church Helps *[RREACH]* International.

A global proclamation ministry, the vision of *RREACH* is to change the way one billion individuals think and hear about the Lord Jesus Christ. Its mission is to proclaim the Lord Jesus Christ worldwide with a strategic burden for strengthening the pastoral leaders and evangelizing the opinion leaders of weaker economies.

From his platform at *RREACH*, Dr. Richard travels throughout the world, clarifying the message of the Bible through lectures and preaching. His audiences are wide-ranging—from non-Christian intellectuals at Harvard to poor pastors in Haiti, from gatherings of a few to a hundred thousand. In recent years he has been speaking to crowds of men in stadiums across the United States on their spiritual responsibilities. The Lord has given him the opportunity of training thousands of church leaders in over seventy countries to preach, live, and think biblically. He also has the privilege of exposing society's "opinion leaders" to the good news of Jesus Christ.

A theologian, preacher, philosopher, evangelist, and author, Dr. Richard holds a Th.D. (in systematic theology) from Dallas Theological Seminary and the Ph.D. (in philosophy) from the University of Delhi. He previously served as the pulpit pastor of the Delhi Bible

Fellowship in New Delhi, India. He chairs the Trainers of Pastors International Coalition [TOPIC]—an international coalition of pastoral training organizations accelerating the training of large numbers of pastoral leaders where the church is growing.

Ramesh, his wife, Bonnie, and their children, Ryan, Robby, and Sitara, live in the Dallas area.

For clarification or information, you may write the author at:
Dallas Theological Seminary
3909 Swiss Avenue
Dallas, TX 75204

For the video version of this book
(gifted to seminary and Bible school libraries
in weaker economies)
please contact
RREACH International
5500 W. Plano Parkway
Plano, TX 75093 USA
Email: info@rreach.org

With humbleness of heart and gratitude toward the Lord, we share with you this resource for your ministry. "All Scripture is God-breathed and is useful for teaching, rebuking, correcting and training in righteousness, so that the man of God may be thoroughly equipped for every good work" (2 Tim. 3:16–17 NIV).

Let me take this opportunity to urge you: "Preach the Word; be prepared in season and out of season; correct, rebuke and encourage—with great patience and careful instruction" (2 Tim. 4:2 NIV). Thank you for investing your life in the proclamation of the Lord Jesus Christ to our world.

In the Inexhaustible One,
Ramesh Richard
President, *RREACH* International
Professor, Dallas Theological Seminary